100 WALKS IN

THE FRENCH ALPS

Also by Terry Marsh

The Summits of Snowdonia
The Mountains of Wales
The Lake Mountains: Volumes 1 and 2
The Pennine Mountains
100 Walks in the French Pyrenees
The Dales Way
A Northern Coast to Coast Walk

British Library Cataloguing in Publication Data

Marsh, Terry
 100 Walks in the French Alps
 I. Title
 796.52209449

ISBN 0 340 57478 X

Typeset by Hewer Text Composition Services, Edinburgh
Printed and bound in Great Britain by BPC Hazell Books Ltd

Hodder and Stoughton Ltd
A Division of Hodder Headline PLC
338 Euston Road
London NW1 3BH

100 WALKS IN

THE FRENCH ALPS

TERRY MARSH

Hodder & Stoughton

LONDON SYDNEY AUCKLAND

FOR PHYL AND JOHN

Acknowledgements

Without the help, tolerance and support of family and friends, and my wife in particular, I could not have completed this book; it seems to have been ever thus, but it lessens not my gratitude.

All photographs are from the Terry Marsh Picture Library. Maps drawn by Ian Sandom.

CONTENTS

THE 100 WALKS

Region 1: CHABLAIS

Region 4: ARAVIS-BORNES-BARGY

Chaîne des Aravis

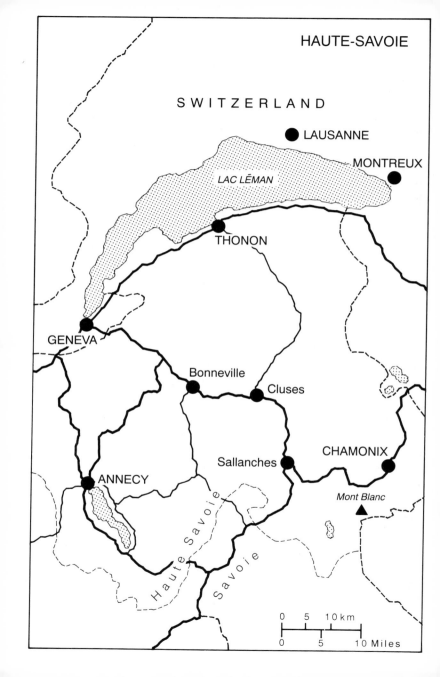

INTRODUCTION

Not surprisingly, given the wealth of literature concentrating on the great snow-capped massif of Mont Blanc, there is a tendency to think of the French Alps only in that context, looking no further, perhaps, than the popular resorts along the Arve valley, among which Chamonix is undoubtedly the most renowned. But it would be wrong to discount the Alps as having nothing of appeal to the ordinary weekend walkers of Britain.

More and more visitors are now finding that beyond the hubbub of the Chamonix valley there exists a vast complex of mountain groups well within the capabilities of walkers nurtured on the hills of Britain. Indeed, along the flanks of the Arve in its mid and lower reaches, and down the side valleys of Montjoie, Arly and the Giffre, are grouped some of the finest mountain walks imaginable.

100 Walks in the French Alps explores these more accessible ranges, offering routes to satisfy walkers of all standards from rugged, high mountain walks from remote refuges, to pleasant lakeside rambles, from energetic ascents of proud peaks, to less demanding assaults on the menus of mountain refuges. At their highest level (Grade A), these predominantly limestone peaks are on a par with the Cuillins of Skye, and the more complex mountains of Torridon and Glencoe, ranging in height from 2000–2500m (6500–8500ft). Lower down the scale comes a splendid tally of walks that will appeal to anyone fit enough to tackle the British hills on a regular basis, providing almost limitless opportunity to explore. Remote, wild valleys, where chamois and bouquetin flit across the grey-green slopes, will appeal to backpackers, as will the long-distance trails of the region, most notably the GR5, the Tour du Mont Blanc and the Tour du Pays du Mont Blanc, though there are more. Entertaining and exciting mountain trails, starting through forest of pine and spruce, and rising to magnificent summits with outstanding scenery, will repay every ounce of effort and determination.

Away from the Mont Blanc massif, though it is impossible to be 'away' from it visually, a less austere landscape awaits; one of rich green alpine meadows, the true 'alps', rising to limestone walls and peaks of great attraction, many retaining snow for most of the year. It is a region of remarkable contrasts, extending (almost) from the shores of Lac Léman (Lake Geneva), south across the *département* of Haute Savoie, spanning the fiercely proud cantons and communities of Chablais, Faucigny, Haut Giffre, Aravis, and Bornes.

The true extent of these mountains is considerably greater than this book allows, for the Alps continue ever southwards towards the Mediterranean, and from the focal point of the Chamonix valley, swing north and east in a great arc across the top of Italy. The walks in this book are all accessible from one base, though that would have to be not far from Sallanches in the mid-section of the Arve valley. From such a base – I used Combloux during the most recent research for the book – it is possible to reach even the remoteness of Abondance, or Fier, in less time than most people travel for their weekend walks at home, and in so doing to explore the Alps in a broader sense, to live and breathe the alpine culture, the elemental freedom of spirit, and the *joie de vivre* these mountains have to offer.

Flora and fauna

The French Alps are a paradise for walkers with any level of interest in natural history. Flowers grow in abundance, visited by an amazing and colourful variety of butterflies and insects, while the afforested slopes provide shelter for a wide range of bird life and animals.

Within Haute Savoie, there are no less than eight nature reserves, four of which are visited by walks in this book –

Aiguilles Rouges, by far the largest and best organised, Sixt, Contamines and Passy. Anyone with the ability to read French will find the *Guide de la Réserve Naturelle des Aiguilles Rouges* a fascinating book, crammed with well-illustrated articles on every aspect of natural history within the reserve. It lists 594 species of plants, 23 mammals, and 84 species of bird found in the reserve, an outstanding range by any standards. Two small, pocket-sized books – *Flore des Montagnes* and *Faune des Montagnes* – will prove a useful aid to identification of the many species which do not occur in Britain. Alas, no one in France seems to have produced a comprehensive book on the butterflies of the region, though quite a few English-language field guides that also cover Europe remedy this deficiency. The best flower months are June, July and August, and the greatest abundance found in the high, sheltered valleys.

June is also the time of year when you might be treated to the sight of young bouquetin, though mothers are understandably very protective. The bouquetin, a relative of the goat, had virtually disappeared from the Alps in the nineteenth century. In Switzerland they had all gone by 1661, and in Austria towards 1800. The last two bouquetin in France were killed on the Mont Blanc massif in 1870. Thankfully, the Italian King Victor Emmanuel I, in 1836, created a nature reserve in the Val d'Aoste, which in 1922 became the Parc National du Grand Paradis. Here, bouquetin survived, and in time the French and Swiss authorities followed the king's lead. Haute Savoie saw the reintroduction of bouquetin between 1967 and 1978, and numbers have now increased to almost 1000.

The rather smaller chamois exist, however, in greater numbers, and can usually be found high on the mountain slopes or in forests to the west and south of the Arve valley. Marmots, too, scurry about everywhere, but you have to be quick to spot them. A large rodent, they live in burrows, and spend the winter months in hibernation. During the last thirty-five years, numbers of marmot were sent from the Alps to colonise the mountains of the Pyrenees, which they have done with outstanding natural ability.

Some of the denser forests are the haunt of wild boars and fallow deer, though both stealth and good fortune will be needed to find any of these. To help with identification, a visit to the animal park at Merlet, not far from Chamonix, is excellent value for money. Here, all these animals, except the wild boar, plus a couple of llamas, roam about freely in a natural setting: if there is a place for zoos in modern society, this is how they should be.

Freedom to roam

There is a general freedom to roam over all open paths and tracks, and across the high mountain slopes, generally throughout the French Alps. But in practice there is little need to do so, every valley and mountainside being furnished with a maze of networked footpaths that make random wandering a meaningless exercise.

Even so, the rules of good behaviour still apply, and no decent walker will leave gates open, trample crops, or damage walls. Smoking, or lighting fires, is forbidden in forests, and the rule actively enforced.

As in Britain, there is a Country Code, the *Code du Randonneur*. Behave sensibly, and you will be tolerated everywhere.

How to get there

By Air

The nearest airport is at Geneva, in Switzerland, and receives many direct flights from UK airports. Cars can be hired at the airport, which is about 1 ½ hours' driving time from Chamonix, mostly on high-speed *autoroutes*. A direct rail service links Geneva and the Arve valley (see below).

By Rail

Renowned for its *Trains à grande vitesse (TGV)*, France has an excellent rail network based on Paris. Good rail services operate between the Channel ports and Paris, while TGV services run to Cluses (for Sallanches, Samoëns, Haut-Giffre and Taninges) and Le Fayet/St Gervais-les-Bains (for Combloux, Megève and Chamonix). Information on rail services in France is available from the French Government Tourist Office (Tel: 071 491 7622) or French Railways (Motorail: Tel: 071 409 3518, or foot passengers: Tel: 0891 515 477).

By Coach

There are a surprising number of express coaches whizzing across France from the UK, running from London and many regional centres. Basic information (and a booking service) is available on Tel: 071 730 0202. The service from London runs each Monday, Wednesday and Friday through the year, leaving at 1530h and arriving in Chamonix next day at 1025h, a journey of just on 19 hours. Return fare (1993) is £97.00.

By Road

These days less arduous than might be supposed, the journey by road, making use of France's superb network of *autoroutes*, is an excellent alternative for groups without very young children. Many trips have now honed my own route to near perfection, and would suit anyone for whom Portsmouth is a convenient port. An overnight Thursday crossing to Le Havre, preferably with sleeping accommodation on board the ferry, leads to an early-morning run to Paris, a brief altercation with the *périphérique*, and a straight run down the A6 for an overnight stay in Beaune, quite by chance a major wine producing area! Some way beyond Beaune, turn along the A40 for Geneva and Chamonix, arriving Saturday midday, when most visitors are either going home or just setting off from the UK. Total driving distance from Le Havre, 530 miles (Beaune = 326 miles). Allow about £30.00 each way for tolls on the *autoroutes*. Anyone wanting a detailed route can write to me c/o the publishers.

In 1994, the Channel Tunnel comes into operation, but will not significantly alter the master plan, though the spell on the Paris *périphérique* will be longer, and the chance of overnight rest while moving ever closer to your destination will be gone.

Accommodation

Gîtes d'Étape

Gîtes d'Étape are rather like unmanned youth hostels for people of all ages, they are inexpensive and found in some out-of-the-way places, making them ideal for walkers seeking some measure of solitude. Some have wardens, who may offer meals, but do not rely on this. They are intended exclusively for walkers, climbers, and cyclists, and should not be confused with Gîtes de France, which are country cottages available for holiday let. Pillows and blankets are usually provided, and the maximum stay is normally three nights. Booking is vital during July and August, and enquiries should be made at the nearest *Office du Tourisme* or *Syndicat d'Initiative*.

Camping

Most campsites in the valleys are excellent, with good amenities, and suitable for long stays. Many have basic shop facilities. However, campsites are popular with French families, and during the main season can be overcrowded and noisy.

Wild camping, backpacker-style, is at its most sublime high

in the mountains, and two sites in the Montjoie valley, above Notre-Dame-de-la-Gorge, have been specifically designated for lightweight campers.

Mountain refuges

Quite a number of mountain refuges are privately-owned, and often provide an excellent 'restaurant' service. Amenities vary, but never fall below a good standard. In the main season they are tremendously popular, and booking is vital.

Where walks would specifically benefit from a stay at a refuge, this has been mentioned in the text. More information about refuges is usually available from the local tourist information offices.

Equipment

The equipment required for the walks in this book is little more than might be used on mountain walks in Britain. At the very least for all but the easiest walks this should comprise comfortable mountain boots with Vibram soles, warm socks, suitable trousers (shorts are fine for warm days, but something more substantial will be needed at altitude and for the evenings), general upper body wear, wind- and waterproof clothing, hat (wide-brimmed, for shade), and gloves. A high-factor sun cream, or glacier cream if you are crossing snow banks, is always a good idea, plus insect repellent and/or analgesic spray, first aid kit, and a good pair of sun-glasses.

Depending on the timing of your visit, crampons and ice-axes may be necessary, but as a rule are not needed from mid-July into August. A rope will come in handy on Grade A walks, and a few of the Grade Bs.

Walkers staying overnight in refuges will need a torch (don't forget spare batteries and bulbs), and, if you are a light sleeper, ear plugs. You may also need sheet liners and indoor shoes.

Emergency food that doesn't melt, maps, compass and whistle complete these fundamental requirements.

Maps

The maps on which this book is based are all at the scale 1:25 000. They are: IGN 'Top 25': 3429 ET: Bonneville–Cluses; IGN 'Top 25': 3430 ET: La Clusaz–Grand-Bornand; IGN 'Top 25': 3528 ET: Morzine–Massif du Chablais; IGN Série Bleue: 3529 Ouest: Taninges; IGN 'Top 25': 3530 ET: Samoëns–Haut-Giffre; IGN 'Top 25': 3531 ET: St-Gervais-les-Bains–Massif du Mont Blanc; IGN 'Top 25': 3531 OT: Megève–Col des Aravis; IGN 'Top 25': 3630 OT: Chamonix–Mont-Blanc

All these maps can be bought in Britain at good booksellers, and a few specialist map sellers advertising in the outdoor press. They will be found, however, to be cheaper to buy in France, if you can afford to leave the detailed planning until you get there. 53FF was the standard price per map in 1993.

Emergencies

The mountain rescue service in the Alps is impressive, both in terms of its efficiency, and its cost. Do not call it out unless you need to.

The first port of call, if an accident occurs in a high or remote part of the region, should, if possible, be a manned refuge, all of which have telephones to the outside world.

Back at valley level, and with access to a public telephone, the number to ring is that for the Police – 17. The Chamonix-based Mountain Rescue Service can be contacted on 50 53 16 89.

Whatever your means of summoning help, do remember to have a map with the precise position of the injured party marked on it: this will help immensely in the event of language difficulties, or if, as is likely, you are unable to re-ascend to the spot.

Weather

The nearer your walk to the Mont Blanc massif, the more it is likely to be affected by Mont Blanc's own 'climate'. Yet only a few miles away, for example along the Chaîne des Aravis, blue skies have been known to contrast with evil, brooding gloom over Mont Blanc – and vice versa.

June to September are the most favourable months, when you can expect more in the way of warm, sunny weather than rain. Even so, my first aborted attempt at climbing Mont Blanc, one September long ago, came at the end of three weeks non-stop torrential rain.

Weather bulletins are posted daily at all tourist information offices, though the influence of Mont Blanc is very real, and far-reaching. Recorded weather forecasts, for those able to speak French, can be obtained on 50 53 03 40. Weather maps (*Météo*) appear in national and local newspapers, and on television, where symbols speak louder than words, much as they do in this country.

About the walks

There are many more walks in the French Alps than this book could hope to contain, certainly more than enough to fill a lifetime of walking. The 100 walks given here are an eclectic choice drawn from more than twenty years of exploration and wandering. Today waymarking cuts down on the element of wandering and most moments of doubt are resolved by the judicious stripes of waymarked routes. Only among the highest summits, the Grade A ascents, is waymarking likely to be missing. Good paths, too, generally abound, and few of the walks in this book venture off the well-trodden path.

But neither waymarking, nor the presence of a fine pathway

network, should lull you into underestimating these walks. Some, but by no means all, of them are extremely demanding. And in the Alps, the difficulties are often more sustained, and escape routes few and far between. So walkers should consider carefully the grade attached to each route to gauge what to expect. If in doubt about your ability, or current state of strength, to continue with a route, do, please, come back down. I've done it often enough, and lived to write about it!

Early in the season, i.e. before mid-July, many of the upper slopes retain snow. If your visit coincides with this period, be sure to take an ice-axe, crampons, and a short length of rope and associated equipment. At all times of the year, be sure to have a plentiful supply of film for your camera, and though there are many mountain refuges at which refreshments are available, do not rely on this, take sufficient supplies of your own.

Grading of Walks

The French Alps offer walks to suit all standards, from family outings to high-level routes demanding the experience of walkers happy to scramble at advanced level, and skilled in the use of ice-axes, ropes, crampons, and in map and compass technique. So you will know what you are letting yourself in for I have employed a rough grading system, and even that is by its very nature subjective. Grades have been combined, or expanded/diminished by using '+' or '–' signs where this gives a better idea.

Most walks tend to be rather longer than in Britain, and need more time to complete. None of them, however, needs to be thought of in terms of the high-altitude mountaineering normally associated with the Alps, though the proximity of the great Mont Blanc massif does have its influence on neighbouring ranges of mountains, notably in its effect on the weather. A number of ascents, by virtue of their difficulty and remoteness, can have a high-mountain feel about them, which could intimidate less experienced walkers.

Grade A These routes, of which there are but a few, and which I hesitate to describe as 'walks' (but have done so for consistency), are suitable only for the experienced (and, preferably, accompanied) mountaineer accustomed to long and strenuous days. You can expect to encounter airy traverses and crests, advanced scrambling bordering on rock climbing, routes which are not always on paths, some snow and, occasionally, glacier work, overnight stays in refuges, and prolonged exercise at heights usually near or in excess of 2500m (8000ft).

Grade B Routes in this category are within the capabilities of any regular and fit weekend walker in Britain accustomed to coping with ascents of the Welsh, Lakeland and Scottish mountains. For some routes the ability to use an ice-axe is essential, as is a willingness to tackle far greater height gains than we are able to in Britain. In the main, however, this is not the case, though walkers should be prepared for long stretches of energetic exercise on most walks. You may find sections that have a sense of exposure, some scrambling (aided and unaided), and the need to cope with short snow slopes. While most of the walks in this group may be accomplished within one day, there is often advantage in staying overnight in refuges, while just a few of the walks are multi-day where this, or a wild camp, is needed.

Grade C Walks, not necessarily low level, within the capability of every fit person; some uphill work, and not always short walks, but capable of being accomplished safely with hands in pockets (figuratively speaking) most of the time.

Walks in this category, but with more than 900m (3000ft) of ascent, are graded C + +.

Grade D Simple lakeside, riverside or gradually-rising valley walks requiring no special equipment, but demanding a modest standard of fitness.

Times

The times given for each walk are a calculation based on (a) personal experience, (b) times given in French guidebooks, and (c) times displayed on the many signposts and information boards, in other words, a realistic average for a fit and healthy walker. Where only one time is given, it is for the whole walk. None of the times makes allowance for stops of any description – time for eating, viewing, taking photographs, exploring, and regaining your breath, should be added.

Heights, distances and ascent

Heights are taken from the IGN 'Top 25' or Série Bleue maps, as is the spelling of mountain names, etc. Conversions to feet are metric heights multiplied by 3.2808. In the absence of grid references, spot heights are sometimes used. Heights expressed in the heading to a walk are the highest point(s) achieved on that walk, and may not be the summit of a mountain.

Distances are rarely given as the nature of the terrain is often a more important factor in the calculation of a walk's duration. Where distances are given, kilometres are converted to miles by multiplying by 0.625.

Ascents, which are useful in gauging the often considerable height gain to be tackled, are measured from the starting point, and include re-ascents encountered en route, both up and down.

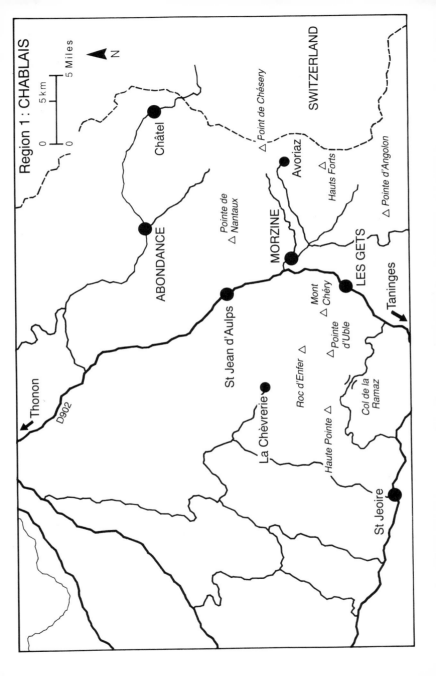

Region 1 : CHABLAIS

N

0   5 km
0   5 Miles

SWITZERLAND

△ Point de Chésery

Châtel

Avoriaz

△ Hauts Forts

△ Pointe d'Angolon

Pointe de △ Nantaux

ABONDANCE

MORZINE

LES GETS

Taninges

St Jean d'Aulps

Mont △ Chéry

△ Pointe d'Uble

Roc d'Enfer △

Col de la Ramaz

La Chèvrerie

Thonon

D902

Haute Pointe △

St Jeoire

REGION 1: CHABLAIS

WALK 1 Pointe de Nantaux (2170m: 7119ft)

Grade:	**B**
Ascent:	**1230m (4035ft)**
Time:	**Ascent: 3h 30–4h. Descent: 2h–2h 30**
Start/Finish:	**Essert la Pierre**
Map:	**IGN 3528 ET: Morzine–Massif du Chablais**

The great green frame of the Pointe de Nantaux rises 6km (3¾ miles) north of the bustling and popular town of Les Gets, deservedly famed for its annual festival of mechanical music. The curiosity is that such a shapely and accessible mountain, lying so close to main mountain thoroughfares, is so neglected. It is, in spite of the many comings and goings around its base, a fine mountain to climb, with a splendid panoramic view from its summit, and heavily flowered alpine pastures to ease the effort of the lower slopes.

The walk begins from the tiny village of Essert la Pierre, just east of the Les Gets–Thonon road (D 902). Locate the village church, and nearby take a wide track on the right heading into woodland. For a while the track runs alongside the Nant Trouble, but gradually distances itself from the stream.

Before long the track forks, and here take a signposted path on the right, finally moving away from the stream altogether. The path climbs fairly energetically to the ruins of the chalets de la Garette, becoming even steeper as it approaches the long, demanding, but immensely satisfying, southwest ridge of the mountain.

The gradient never really eases, and in the last kilometre the broad grassy ridge narrows quite significantly. At Point 1994 you are on the rim of the northwest flank of the mountain, and the ensuing ridge swings round to the east and northeast, narrowing to a fine arête for the final approach to the summit.

WALK 2 Pointe de Chésery (2251m: 7385ft)

Also known as the Pointe de Bécret, and lying on the frontier with Switzerland, the Pointe de Chésery offers two lines of approach from the west. Which is chosen will largely be influenced by one's base: Walk 2a is best approached from Châtel to the north, while Walk 2b comes in from Montriond and Les Lindarets, to the west.

The view from the summit, particularly to the south, is splendid, embracing the summits of Les Hauts Forts (Walk 3) and the Pointe de Vorlaz.

Though less likely to be as extensively affected as higher summits further south, the Pointe de Chésery does often retain snow in its upper reaches well into spring and early summer; if these conditions prevail, an ice-axe will be essential.

2a Col de Bassachaux

Grade:	**B**
Ascent:	**473m (1552ft)**
Time:	**Ascent: 2h. Descent: 1h 30**
Start/Finish:	**Col de Bassachaux, approached by serpentine mountain road from Châtel (12km: 7½ miles) in the Abondance valley**
Map:	**IGN 3528 ET: Morzine–Massif du Chablais**

From the Col de Bassachaux follow the gently rising arête running southeast, dotted with pine trees, to the Tête de Lindaret. Beyond this minor top, the ridge continues in much the same direction, until it reaches, and goes along, the Crête des Rochassons. A final flourish, ascending a wide grassy hollow, rises steeply to the summit, and requires care both on the ascent and the descent in poor conditions, or if still covered with snow.

2b Les Lindarets and the Col de Chésery

Grade:	**B**
Ascent:	**755m (2477ft)**
Time:	**Ascent: 2h 30–3h. Descent: 2h**
Start/Finish:	**Les Lindarets**
Map:	**IGN 3528 ET: Morzine–Massif du Chablais**

A slightly longer approach, heading first for the Col de Chésery on the Franco-Swiss frontier, before doubling back to join Walk 2a at the Crête des Rochassons for the final assault on the summit.

Directly beneath the cables of the Télécabine d'Ardent, a path leaves the minor mountain road (D 338), and heads into the Lécherette valley where a profusion of *télésièges* rather clutter the summer scene. Once beyond these mechanical monsters the valley improves considerably as the path leads towards the chalets at Le Brochau. Before reaching this point, take a track left to the Col de Chésery.

Due north the Pointe de Chésery presents a soaring challenge of rocky ridges which are best ignored. Opt instead for a stretch along the GR5, one of the most popular long-distance walks in this part of France. The rocky ground near the Col de Chésery soon gives way to typically alpine pastures, descending slightly, before leaving the GR5 for a path that climbs to join the Crête des Rochassons. Here it meets Walk 2a, for the final, exciting approach to the summit.

WALK 3 Les Hauts Forts (2466m: 8090ft)

As befits the highest point in Chablais, Les Hauts Forts does not give up its secrets easily, and its ascent lies within the province of experienced mountaineers and walkers skilled and comfortable on rock and in exposed places. Snow quite often lingers in the upper corries until well into summer, and when this is the case, an ice-axe as well as a length of rope are indispensable. The shorter of the two principal ascents, from

Avoriaz, is also the more demanding, though it is easy to develop a feeling of false confidence by the comparatively easy going on this valley approach. The ascent from Le Crêt is considerably safer, though it has its moments, but is much longer. It does, however, sport a fine, long ridge, with only one hiccough, the Col de l'Encarnette, to mar otherwise steady progress. Being unenclosed for much of the way, this line of ascent has much better views of the surroundings peaks and valleys.

From the summit, the view east, into Switzerland, and south, is especially impressive, and wisely to be contemplated for as long as possible before making the descent.

3a From Avoriaz

Grade:	**A**
Ascent:	**652m (2139ft)**
Time:	**Ascent: 2h 30–3h. Descent: 2h–2h 30**
Start/Finish:	**Avoriaz**
Map:	**IGN 3528 ET: Morzine–Massif du Chablais**

Start from Avoriaz, leaving by the path that begins at the téléphérique station, and follow this in a southerly direction, generally keeping in line with the cable-lift pylons. As the gradient increases, so the path snakes about to ease the upward progress, arriving finally directly below the summit of Les Hauts Forts, from where, at first, it seems unattainable.

A steep slope, Le Plan Brasy, ensues, often retaining snow, requiring great care at the best of times, and physically demanding. This leads to a narrow constriction between two rock walls by means of which the summit ridge can be reached. Once on the ridge, follow it west. It becomes very narrow and exposed in places, at least as far as a brèche, or gap, which can be passed with care on the south. Beyond the gap, a short and awkward rock wall is all that remains before the summit is finally reached.

3b From Le Crêt

Grade:	**B+**
Ascent:	**1365m (4478ft)**
Time:	**Ascent: 4h–4h 30. Descent: 2h 30–3h**
Start/Finish:	**Le Crêt, in the vallée de la Manche, southwest of Morzine**
Map:	**IGN 3528 ET: Morzine–Massif du Chablais**

Le Crêt, a small hamlet, lies down the long valley running southeast from Morzine, on a small side road. From the eastern end of the village cross a field to the right of a stream and find a pathway at the edge of the forest. The route through the forest is remorselessly uphill, passes some ruined chalets, and continues to those at Bramaturtaz (1525m: 5003ft). A short while later you cross the stream and the path continues to climb across open mountain pasturage to the Chalets du Plan de Zore, from where it is possible to gain the mountain ridge ahead, at the Col du Pic à Talon (2041m: 6696ft).

From the Col du Pic à Talon the onward route, eastwards, is fairly evident, though the summit still lies 2km (1.2 miles) distant. The route continues to climb as far as the Col de l'Encarnette. Approaching the Col, descend initially to the left, then come back to the Col itself. From there climb the opposing ridge, and follow this, at times surprisingly generous of girth, all the way to the summit.

WALK 4 Lac de Montriond (1067m: 3500ft)

Grade:	**D**
Ascent:	**None**
Time:	**1h**
Start/Finish:	**Picnic area at the eastern end of the lake**
Map:	**IGN 3528 ET: Morzine – Massif du Chablais**

A simple lakeside stroll set in splendid scenery dominated by the Pointe de Nantaux, this walk requires nothing in the way of

Lac de Montriond and the Roc d'Enfer

ropes, crampons, ice-axes, or even walking boots – trainers will do fine. The Lac de Montriond is enormously popular for bathing and sailing, and even on the gloomiest of days there is no prospect of enjoying the walk in total peace and quiet, but it remains an invigorating trek around the lake, lying beneath steep, tree-clad hillsides, and very early in the morning is a refreshing circuit.

The eastern end of the lake is a better starting point, being marginally less popular, and having room to park and a bar-restaurant close by. The view down the length of the lake is quite stunning, with the Roc d'Enfer consuming the whole of the western vista.

It matters not whether you walk clockwise or anticlockwise;

the former has the advantage of shade, especially early in the day, while the northern shore of the lake receives all the sun. The route is perfectly self-evident, the greatest problem likely to be met with is in avoiding the many prone bodies in various stages of undress.

WALK 5 Pointe de Ressachaux (2173m: 7129ft)

Grade:	**B**
Ascent:	**1123m (3684ft)**
Time:	**Ascent: 3h 30–4h. Descent: 2h 30**
Start/Finish:	**Minor road in the Vallée de la Manche, near La Grangette**
Map:	**IGN 3528 ET: Morzine–Massif du Chablais**

This relatively quiet peak, the ascent of which is quite rough and tiring, nevertheless commands a magnificent view of Les Hauts Forts, the highest summit in the massif of Chablais. The mountain, as a result of this lack of attention, is well populated with sheep, goats and chamois.

Along a minor road in the vallée de la Manche, between La Mernaz and La Grangette, it is possible to park in a few places. Just before La Grangette, a signposted footpath heads abruptly into forest, with which it then has an energetic affair for some time, climbing eventually to a wide upland pasture, a great hollow, dotted with chalets, the Combe de Creux.

Gradually, the Pointe de Ressachaux eases into view as the trees are left behind. After the last of the chalets the route bears obliquely left, ascending a grassy flank of the mountain, slowly to pursue an obvious route to the summit.

A return may be made by the same route, but for a slight variation you can descend in a southeastward direction to just below Point 2164, and there swing southwest on a neat ridge, eventually to rejoin the Combe de Creux and the outward route.

WALK 6 Haute Pointe from La Chèvrerie (1958m: 6424ft)

Grade:	**C +**
Ascent:	**840m (2755ft)**
Time:	**Ascent: 3h–3h 30. Descent: 2h 30**
Start/Finish:	**La Chèvrerie**
Map:	**IGN Série Bleue 3529 Ouest: Taninges**

Haute Pointe lies at the western end of a long ridge of mountains, culminating in the formidable Roc d'Enfer, north of the ski resort of Praz de Lys. This, and the ensuing fourteen walks, provide enough walking around Praz de Lys and the adjacent valleys to occupy two leisurely weeks, or one week of more energetic walking, linking summits together. The contrast between rocky peaks and pinnacles and the soft green alpine pastures around their base is everywhere vivid and enticing, while many of the lakes offer simple, undemanding excursions across alpine meadows richly hued with wild flowers, and echoing loudly to the ever-present clanging of *clochettes*.

Beyond the Haute Pointe–Roc d'Enfer ridge lies the wooded Brevon valley, from where a number of the walks begin. Here, just east of the Lac de Vallon, La Chèvrerie is a fine base from which to explore the northern fringes of the range.

Begin from La Chèvrerie along the trail ascending into the Vallon de Bellecombe, ignoring, not far from the start, that heading for the Forêt de Pététoz. In due course, cross the Bellecombe stream and continue to the road-end at Plan des Rasses. To this point the road is motorable, but rough, and the start from La Chèvrerie is preferable.

Beyond the chalet at Plan des Rasses, a path crosses the stream and rises steeply into forest, working a way around the unseen, tree-clad spur of the Rocher de la Boucle, finally to emerge from the trees near Chavan. Now ascend rather more easily to the Col de Chavan.

Beyond the col a wide grassy corrie basin spills southwards. This is where the onward route lies, not, as might be supposed, along the ridge to the west. The continuation from the col, however, does start westwards along the arête for a short distance, before moving out, descending slightly, across the combe. Once across the combe, climb to a small col, with Haute Pointe just above, to the west, and from there ascend to the summit, a fine and popular vantage point.

The best return to La Chèvrerie is by the outward route.

WALK 7 Haute Pointe from the Col de la Ramaz (1958m: 6424ft)

Grade:	**C**
Ascent:	**446m (1463ft)**
Time:	**Ascent: 1h 30. Descent: 1h**
Start/Finish:	**Col de la Ramaz**
Map:	**IGN Série Bleue 3529 Ouest: Taninges**

This is the easiest approach to Haute Pointe, little more than a gently rising stroll in the early stages, but the whole walk should not be underestimated, particularly as the summit is approached.

From the Col de la Ramaz, where there is ample parking, head down the road in the direction of Sommant, and after 500m take a broad track on the right, ascending steadily towards an isolated chalet just beneath the Col de Chavan. Once the col is reached, start along the arête to the west, leaving it after 200m to begin a traverse of the wide corrie basin below Haute Pointe. Aim for a small col, just east of the summit, from where it may then be easily reached.

Return by the outward route.

WALK 8 Tour de la Haute Pointe (Col de Cordon: 1636m: 5367ft. Col north of Haute Pointe: 1815m: 5955ft. Col de Chavan: 1757m: 5764ft. Haute Pointe: 1958m: 6424ft)

Grade:	**C +**
Ascent:	**797m (2615ft)**
Time:	**3h–3h 30**
Start/Finish:	**Refuge de Sommant**
Map:	**IGN Série Bleue 3529 Ouest: Taninges**

It is a matter of some Gallic pride whether one's heritage lies within Chablais or Faucigny, and for one not brought up on these matters no amount of questioning will ever produce agreement among locals on where the boundaries between the two exist. Because the whole of the massif around Praz de Lys has, in the Pointe de Marcelly, a toe-hold in the Giffre valley, at Taninges, and, at the northern edge, has its feet firmly planted in Chablais, the high mountain road passing the ski

Female bouquetin

station at Sommant and running down to Praz de Lys has been used as an arbitrary, convenient and non-contentious boundary.

The ascent of Haute Pointe is detailed in Walks 6 and 7, but for those who want to see more of the surrounding countryside, a very laudable idea, there is a fine circuit of the mountain, starting from Sommant, where the main road swings north and a minor road runs on to the Refuge de Sommant (restaurant/buvette). Park here.

Return to the main road and follow this as if heading for the Col de la Ramaz, but leaving it after 200m for a path running behind chalets. The path climbs easily across flower-laden meadows to the Col de Cordon, situated near the Pointe de Rovagne.

Cross the col and descend into the combe beyond, ignoring a road branching left, and continuing to the Chalets des Charmettes seen ahead on the flanks of a low ridge, and gained by a slight ascent. From the chalets move northeast, keeping to the right of the ridge, and heading for another col, just north of Haute Pointe, not named on maps.

Beyond this second col, the route descends quite steeply for a while beneath the Pointe de Chavannais until it meets the path ascending from the Plan des Rasses (Walk 6), which should be followed to the Col de Chavan. Both Walks 6 and 7 describe the means by which Haute Pointe itself may be ascended (add 1 hour for the return journey from the Col de Chavan).

From the Col de Chavan descend steeply to a rough road-end serving an isolated chalet, and follow this out to the main mountain road at Ramaz, there taking the minor road past Farquet to the Refuge de Sommant.

WALK 9 Col des Follys (1652m: 5420ft. Unnamed summit: 1690m: 5545ft) and the Vallée de la Chèvrerie

Grade:	**C**
Ascent:	**572m (1877ft)**
Time:	**3h 30–4h**
Start/Finish:	**La Chèvrerie (Pont-de-la-Joux)**
Map:	**IGN Série Bleue 3529 Ouest: Taninges**

Gained by a narrow valley at La Clusaz, La Chèvrerie lies very much at the heart of Chablais. Here, on the flanks of the Roc d'Enfer, rises the source of the River Brevon, which later joins the Dranse on the final stage of its journey to Lac Léman. The head of the valley ends abruptly in the soaring peaks of the Roc d'Enfer (Walk 13), but in the lower reaches, where forest drapes the hillsides, less demanding walking is available.

Continue through La Chèvrerie and take the forest trail heading for the Pont-de-la-Joux where cars may be parked. From here a path, heading ultimately for the Roc d'Enfer, sets off northeast to the Chal d'en Haut, beyond which it zizgags through the forest to more chalets at Le Torchon. Here you leave the forest for a while, as the route climbs steadily across alpine pastures to the Col des Follys. At the Col, there is a fine view of the Roc d'Enfer.

A path runs along the crest south of the Col des Follys, crossing a minor summit, and you should follow this for a few hundred metres, but leave it at the next minor col for a path descending, right, into forest once more and making for Le Grand Souvroz, just above the forest edge.

From Le Grand Souvroz a forest trail descends westwards, and then north westwards to Les Favières, returning leisurely through the forest to Pont-de-la-Joux.

WALK 10 Pointe de Chavasse (2012m: 6600ft)

Grade:	**C +**
Ascent:	**467m (1532ft)**
Time:	**Ascent: 2hr–2h 30. Descent: 1h 30–2h**
Start/Finish:	**Parking, near Col de la Ramaz**

Retrospective from the summit of Pointe de Chavasse

Map: **IGN Série Bleue 3529 Ouest: Taninges**

The long mountain ridge linking the summits of the Roc d'Enfer and Haute Pointe, though difficult (if not impossible) to complete as a ridge walk, being too broken for that, nevertheless provides a number of excellent walks to summits that are fine viewpoints and worthy of anyone's attention.

From the parking area near the Col de la Ramaz take the broad track (signposted: 'Col de Chalune, 'Col de Foron'), heading for the three isolated buildings that comprise the Chalet Blanc. Immediately behind the chalet the Pointe de Chalune is a great temptation (Walk 12), and the onward track is signposted towards it. For the Pointe de Chavasse, however, the shallow green valley running northwest, terminating in the Col de Vésinaz, is what you need.

Leave the Chalet Blanc, following the obvious trail, but leaving it at a signpost for a narrow path aiming for the Col de Vésinaz. Towards the col the gradient steepens a little, and a couple of small zigzags ease progress. Above the zigzags, keep to the right, rather than following a more tempting path going left, and ascend to the col which, surprisingly, boasts a green turnstile. Beyond the turnstile grassy banks provide a comfortable perch from which to gaze down on the Forêt de Pététoz and to the Brevon valley.

Returning to the turnstile, follow a distinct path ascending beneath some daunting cliffs and pinnacles, which for a long time have given the impression that here is the summit of the mountain. Thankfully, this is not so, since they represent a formidable and friable challenge to all but sheep and chamois, and even the sheep prefer the shade on the northerly side.

The path climbs a broad rock step to a shallow corrie basin, with the path running out across it to a grassy ridge. Higher on the right, however, and immediately to the left of the rocky pinnacles, a shallow col can be reached by ascending loose scree (not unduly demanding, but requiring care). From the col, at which the true summit of the mountain springs into view, climb left on an undulating path leading to a twin-topped grassy summit. The first summit appears to be the higher.

From this modest vantage point, the view extends across Lac Léman to the Jura Mountains in Switzerland, though the eastward view is closed by the fractured pinnacles of Pointe de Chalune. Haute Pointe lies a short distance away, and the connecting ridge, far below, is very inviting, but although some local guidebooks suggest a connection to the ridge, I have yet to find it other than in the form of a precarious descent of a grassy couloir, not to be recommended.

A leisurely return should be made by the outward route.

WALK 11 Pointe de Chalune (2116m: 6942ft) from La Chèvrerie

Grade:	**C + +**
Ascent:	**998m (3274ft)**
Time:	**Ascent: 3h 30. Descent: 2h 30**
Start/Finish:	**La Chèvrerie (Pont-de-la-Joux)**
Map:	**IGN Série Bleue 3529 Ouest: Taninges**

The Pointe de Chalune is a fine, inviting peak sandwiched between the Roc d'Enfer and the Pointe de Chavasse, and may be ascended both from the north, the Brevon valley, and the south, the Col de la Ramaz (Walk 12).

In the Brevon valley continue through La Chèvrerie and on to a forest trail leading to the Pont-de-la-Joux, where cars may

Pointe de Chalune

be parked. Continue on a wide forest track, passing Le Finge and Les Favières to reach Souvroz d'en Bas, deep in the forest. The track here swings southwards, heading into a rising valley along the Souvroz stream, and reaching Souvroz du Milieu, due west of the Roc d'Enfer. From here continue ascending, rather more steeply, to reach the Col de Foron.

From the Col there is a splendid view of the ridge leading up to the Roc d'Enfer (Walk 13), but for Pointe de Chalune, the direction lies across the Col de Foron to the Col de Chalune. Continue from the Col de Chalune, west of north, on a rough path along which, from time to time, simple scrambling will necessitate the use of hands. Gradually, the direction becomes more westerly, and the ridge narrows quite sharply with steep drops on both sides, before finally reaching the summit. Close by, the eastern face of the mountain is particularly abrupt, and though its summit affords an excellent panoramic view across Chablais, caution is advised if approaching the edge.

A simple retreat by the outward route is perfectly feasible, but a more enterprising alternative is at hand. This will only marginally extend the overall time.

Return to the Col de Chalune, and take an infrequently used, but distinct, path which contours, west–southwest, across the southern flank of the mountain, in the direction of the Col de Vésinaz. This strikes the southwest ridge of the Pointe de Chalune, a fine grassy arête, some way above the col. At this point, cross the arête and descend to gain a path running down the upper reaches of Pététoz. From the Chalets de Pététoz it is easy to follow a forest trail back to the starting point. A more direct, but not obvious line follows the wooded crest back to Lajoux, while another alternative lopes off to seek out the Lac de Pététoz, rejoining the main forest trail lower down.

WALK 12 Pointe de Chalune (2116m: 6942ft) from Col de la Ramaz

Grade:	**C+**
Ascent:	**571m (1873ft)**
Time:	**Ascent: 1h 30–2h. Descent: 1h–1h 30**
Start/Finish:	**Parking, near Col de la Ramaz**
Map:	**IGN Série Bleue 3529 Ouest: Taninges**

From the parking area near the Col de la Ramaz take the signposted track heading for the Chalet Blanc and the Col de Foron. The Chalet, a small group of isolated farm buildings, lies directly beneath the Pointe de Chalune. From the Chalet, a path continues a short distance to a signpost, and from here follow the increasingly steep path to the Col de Chalune and a

Heading for the Chalet Blanc: Pointe d'Uble on the right

fine view of the long ridge rising from the Col de Foron to the Roc d'Enfer.

From the Col de Chalune continue west of north, on a rough path, interspersed with short rocky moments when the use of hands will be needed. Gradually, as the direction turns to the west, the ridge narrows appreciably with sharp drops on both flanks, before finally reaching the summit.

The abrupt east face of the mountain is close by, and should only be approached with caution.

The simplest return is by the outward route, but, extending the walk by about an hour, it is possible from the Col de Chalune to follow a good path across the southern flank of the mountain to a grassy spur extending out to Point 1879, just above the Col de Vésinaz. Once you reach this spur, follow it down to the Col de Vésinaz, and there turn left, southeast, following a distinct path that descends directly to the Chalet Blanc to rejoin the outward route.

WALK 13 Roc d'Enfer (2243m: 7359ft)

Grade:	A/B
Ascent:	745m (2444ft)
Time:	Ascent: 3h 30–4h. Descent: 3h
Start/Finish:	Parking, near Col de la Ramaz
Map:	IGN Série Bleue 3529 Ouest: Taninges

For a mountain of modest stature, the Roc d'Enfer (the Rock of Hell), dominates much of the surrounding countryside, and is very aptly named. Its ascent is a magnificent and exhilarating undertaking, but demands considerable expertise and confidence. The summit ridge, a long and very exposed affair, is dangerous both when snow lingers along it, and after prolonged rain, and there have been a number of fatal accidents on the mountain. A length of rope and a few slings and karabiners could prove useful along the middle section of the ridge.

Roc d'Enfer and the ski resort of Praz de Lys

The walk makes use of the altitude of the Col de la Ramaz as a starting point, and this, unless content with climbing to the south summit, involves a two-way crossing of the intervening arête. Competent and experienced walkers will find it extremely entertaining, but it is no place to relax concentration.

From the Col de la Ramaz follow Walk 12 (Pointe de Chalune) as far as the Col de Chalune, and continue from there descending slightly to the Col de Foron. From this col, a long sloping, grassy and alluring arête leads via the Tête de Charseuvre towards the southern face of the mountain. Eventually, the path reaches the foot of a rocky couloir, and by ascending this (its left edge is marginally more feasible) you can reach the summit ridge. Continue along the ridge and on to the northern flank to circumvent a rocky promontory, where snow often lingers. Once beyond this obstacle the ridge continues to the southern summit without much more ado.

The continuation to the principal summit involves a long, exposed ridge walk, with a reputation for severity, and on which there are a few delicate moments of passage.

The ridge soon reaches a brèche, beyond which you climb a rock step, using fixed cables. From there a long, undulating knife-edge runs on towards the main summit. Near the summit the path moves to the northern side of the mountain again, a delicate passage along which pitons have been fixed for security. This section becomes highly dangerous if snow is still present, when it should be avoided. Beyond it you join a path ascending from the village of Graydon and this, finally, leads to the summit. The distance between the two summits is little more than 500m, but it consumes much in the way of time, energy and concentration. Anyone reluctant to make the return journey is advised to descend to Graydon, and resolve the transport difficulties from there.

WALK 14 Pointe d'Uble (1963m: 6440ft)

Grade:	C +
Ascent:	**795m (2608ft)**
Time:	**Ascent: 3h. Descent: 2h**
Start/Finish:	**300m north of Les Côtes, northwest of the Pont des Gets**
Map:	**IGN Série Bleue 3529 Ouest: Taninges**

Very much overshadowed by the presence of its near, and higher, neighbours, Pointe d'Uble nevertheless provides a delightful and energetic walk, quite often with the benefit of solitude.

The way begins at a hairpin bend just north of Les Côtes, and west of Praz de Lys. From here walk along the motorable trail that leaves the hairpin bend initially in a northerly direction, and follow this through a steep-sided and wooded valley following the Boutigny stream. The road terminates near the Chalets de la Crotte, from where a path climbs steeply to more chalets at Rosset.

From Rosset take a path heading right that soon rises to tackle a rock outcrop beyond which lies the steep, sloping lower pastures of Pointe d'Uble. Across these meadows the path soon reaches Perrières, there heading north (and up) once more to pass around woodland, now heading east to gain a long, broad ridge dropping south-southeast from the summit. Ascend this for a short distance, and then swing out across the southern slopes of the mountain to reach another ridge, this time the south-southwest arête.

Pointe d'Uble, with the Roc d'Enfer beyond

This switching from ridge to ridge serves to ease the ascent, and once the south-southwest arête is reached only a straight-forward ascent to the summit remains; the ridge narrows a little as height is gained, but presents no real difficulties.

A return may be made by the same route, or, by leaving the outward route at the south-southeast ridge, you can descend southeast to the Chalet de Parteset. From there continue northwards to the upper edge of the forest where a forest trail leads down to the Vallon de Foron, meeting the D328 about one mile north of the starting point.

WALK 15 Mont Chéry (1826m: 5990ft)

Grade:	C
Ascent:	**690m (2264ft)**
Time:	**Ascent: 3h. Descent: 2h**
Start:	**Les Gets (Le Bénévix)**
Finish:	**Les Gets (Centre)**
Map:	**IGN 3528 ET: Morzine – Massif du Chablais**

This pleasant, circular walk over Mont Chéry is well worth doing, and gives a fine view of the Roc d'Enfer, Pointe de Nantaux and Pointe de Nyon. It is a popular walk, and the mountain is draped in the paraphernalia of skiing by means of which the complete ascent may be accomplished in a matter of minutes, at a price.

Le Bénévix is a small suburb of Les Gets, and from it a path heads between houses to gain the southern slopes of the mountain. Passing beneath an electricity cable it climbs through woodland, and shortly heads southwest to meet a minor road near Le Bouchet. Follow this right, to its end where another path takes up the onward route, crossing stream beds and the ruins at Evois, and continuing past Les Platons and out as far as the small hamlet of Le Mont Caly.

Northeast, a broad grassy ridge rises from Le Mont Caly

without interruption, save for a couple of minor cols, directly to the summit of the mountain.

Descend in an easterly direction, following part of the local Tour des Portes du Soleil, as far as a minor road, where a network of paths and roads facilitates an easy return to Les Gets.

Pointe de Nyon

WALK 16 Pointe de Nyon (2019m: 6624ft)

Grade:	**C +**
Ascent:	**595m (1952ft)**
Time:	**Ascent: 1h–1h 30. Descent: 1h**
Start/Finish:	**Téléski de Lavouet station on a minor road northwest of the summit**
Map:	**IGN 3528 ET: Morzine – Massif du Chablais, or IGN 3530 ET: Samoëns – Haut-Giffre**

The northern slopes of Pointe de Nyon are popular with skiers in winter, evidenced by the proliferation of cable and associated ironmongery. In summer this minor summit remains a fine, short excursion with a good view across the Gets and Morzine valleys.

From the Téléski de Lavouet, located on a minor road leaving the main mountain road between Morzine and Samoëns near Le Grand Pré, follow the path that flanks across the northwest slopes of the mountain. Before long this branches, and the left fork leads across the wide northern corrie basin to the steep edge overlooking the Vallée de la Manche, from where it begins a steep pull to the summit, on which an orientation table identifies many of the surrounding heights.

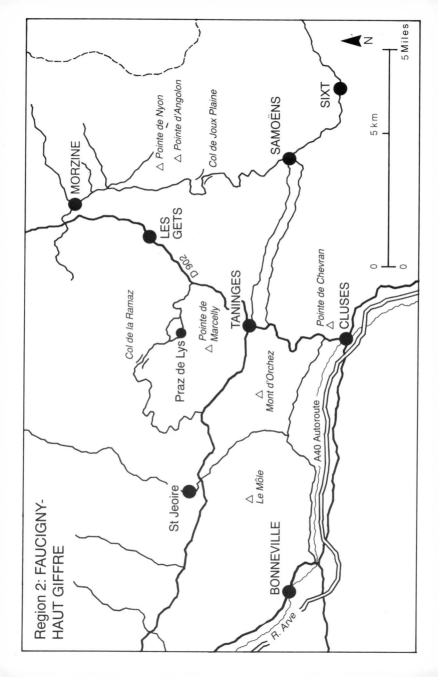

Region 2: FAUCIGNY-HAUT GIFFRE

REGION 2: FAUCIGNY–HAUT-GIFFRE

WALK 17 Pointe d'Angolon (2090m: 6857ft)

Grade	C
Ascent	**400m (1312ft)**
Time:	**Ascent: 1h–1h 30. Descent: 1h**
Start/Finish:	**Lac de Joux Plaine, on the minor road between Samoëns and Morzine**
Map:	**IGN 3530 ET: Samoëns–Haut-Giffre**

Though modest of stature, the Pointe d'Angolon (sometimes referred to as Pointe de Nant Golon) is the highest point of a fine, if brief, ridge walk, and gives a grandstand view of the summits of Pointe de Ressachaux (Walk 5) and Les Hauts Forts (Walk 3), the highest point in the massif of Chablais. There is, too, a fine view of the distant Swiss peaks, swinging round across the Aiguilles Rouges that rise above the Arve valley, and to the Mont Blanc massif itself.

The key to the ascent is a small lake, with attendant bar-restaurant, the Lac de Joux Plaine, lying on the twisting mountain road that links Samoëns and Morzine. Not surprisingly, the lake is a popular spot, particularly at weekends, though the undoubted appeal of the Pointe d'Angolon, the highest point of which cannot be seen from the lake, is something most visitors find easy to resist. As a result, you can enjoy the walk in comparative peace and quiet.

From the lake take a broad track to the obvious Col de Joux Plaine, a short distance away. The col is a slight depression in a low grassy ridge that should now be followed eastwards to gain a ski piste climbing into a wide grassy hollow. Follow the piste until it ends, and from there continue on a steeply ascending narrow path to gain the ridge near a téléski terminus. The view that awaits arrival at the ridge, hitherto hidden from us, is quite outstanding, and surprisingly expansive for so lowly a summit.

Pointe d'Angolon

From the ridge, at spot height 2010, you can see that Pointe d'Angolon has two summits. Head east of north along the ridge, narrow and grassy, to the first summit, passing a short rock wall on the left (though it is climbable), taking care on a short passage of shaly rock. Beyond the first summit, a narrow linking crest runs across to the slightly higher main summit, topped by a cairn, from which Lac Léman (Lake Geneva) can be seen in the far distance. Les Hauts Forts is an especially impressive mountain from this angle.

A retreat by the upward route is the quickest way back to the Lac de Joux Plaine, but by continuing along the ridge from the point at which you joined it, you can make a short, steep descent to an obvious col just below Pointe de Chamossière from where there is an easy return to the lake.

Determined souls can continue further, crossing Pointe de Chamossière, and on as far as the minor summit, La Bourgeoise. At many points paths run away from this narrow crest in the general direction of the Lac de Joux Plaine, effectively allowing you to call it a day when you have had enough.

WALK 18 Refuge Tornay (1763m: 5784ft). Col de Bostan (2290m: 7513ft). Tête de Bostan (2406m: 7894ft) and Col de la Golèse (1671m: 5482ft)

Grade	B
Ascent	1310m (4298ft)
Time:	7h–9h
Start/Finish:	Les Allamands, 5km north of Samoëns
Map:	IGN 3530 ET: Samoëns–Haut-Giffre

The noisy bustle of nearby Samoëns, especially on its Wednesday market day, sharply contrasts with the vast expanse of wild and rugged countryside that stands at its door in the far reaches of the Haut-Giffre. Here, amid steep, wooded valleys and rugged mountain crests the strong and enterprising walker will find exercise and grandeur to match any in the Alps. The frontier peaks of Mont Ruan and Pic de Tenneverge stand not far away, and though these are bounty only for experienced mountaineers, in the countless radiating valleys and ridges there is walking of the grandest kind.

Five kilometres north of Samoëns, in the Clévieux valley, a tributary of the Giffre, lies the tiny hamlet of Les Allamands, a quiet farming village, probably named after the Germanic tribe, the Alamani, which was vanquished in the 5th century. A short distance to the north, near a parking place, a signposted route heads into the Forêt de Bossetan (Bostan) bound for the Refuge Tornay. The path finally emerges from the forest 345m (1130ft) higher, and begins a long and serpentine approach to the Refuge, passing en route the

Chalets de Bostan. Walkers in no hurry will find that an ascent to the Refuge late in the afternoon for an overnight stay will have them tackling the surrounding ridges the next day with renewed vigour. Such a plan would need a reservation at the Refuge (Telephone: 50 90 10 94).

From the Refuge follow the rough path that runs up this steep-sided valley, beneath the crags of the Dents d'Oddaz to the south. There is very little let-up in the gradual climb to the Col de Bostan, and though the route is seldom in doubt it becomes quite rough, even steeper, and may hold hard, crusted snow below the col until early summer: in these conditions crampons as well as an ice-axe could prove life-saving equipment. The Pointe de la Golette is the great peak to the south of the col, available to experienced mountaineers, but likely to be rather intimidating to others.

From the col you can return by the outward route, but a fine continuation lies northwest and west, climbing across the southern flank of the Tête des Verdets to a narrow col, and from there up to the slightly higher Tête de Bostan, the highest point on this circuit. This short stretch between the Col and the Tête de Bostan is a high mountain skiing route, and though on a path, needs care in poor weather conditions.

From the Tête de Bostan the way lies all downhill, flowing (comparatively) effortlessly down to the Refuge and Col de la Golèse. The col, a narrow pass at the foot of the craggy and fragile escarpments of the Pointe de la Golèse, lies on an important migratory route for birds, and has yielded many interesting records to ornitholigsts. Over a 25-year period some 120,000 birds have been caught and ringed. So great is the passage of birds, however, that only 3,000 were caught again. Yet, as in human society, there is always one that has to be different: one blue tit, very much a creature of habit, has been recaptured each year for seven years!

At the Col de la Golèse you join the GR5, and this heads

down to meet the valley of the Giffre. Not far beyond La Batsaz the route joins a roadway, following this towards the chalets, Les Chavonnes. The massive corrie northwest of Les Chavonnes leads up to Pointe d'Angolon (Walk 17). From Les Chavonnes the walk finishes by road, back to the car park near Les Allamands.

WALK 19 Refuge de Folly (1558m: 5111ft) and the Lac des Chambres (2090m: 6857ft)

Grade:	C++
Ascent:	1200m (3937ft)
Time:	Ascent: 3h 30. Descent: 2h
Start/Finish:	Parking, Pont du Pied de Crêt, northeast of Samoëns
Map:	IGN 3530 ET: Samoëns–Haut-Giffre

The Lac des Chambres, often frozen over, lies at the edge of a long, narrow valley that itself frequently retains snow, in addition to its permanent glaciers, well into the summer season. Not surprisingly, the evidence of the long-retreated glaciers is all around in the form of smooth-planed rock outcrops and isolated boulder erratics. What is not so evident is that the whole of this vast region is honeycombed by a network of subterranean passages; indeed the cave of Jean-Bernard, lying just off-route between the Refuge de Folly and the Lac des Chambres, claims the distinction of being the deepest and most substantial cave systems so far discovered in the world. Plunging to a depth of some 1605m (5266ft) from its surface entry point at 1850m, the system then contrives to link a series of caves and crevices extending for 13 km (8+ miles).

As you leave Samoëns by the suburb/village of Les Moulins, a minor road ascends into a tributary valley of the Giffre, reaching a parking place near the Pont du Pied du Crêt. From here a path descends slightly, and crosses the meadows of Le Latay to reach the afforested slopes of the Grands Bois, through which twenty-six zigzags contrive to ease progress to the hanging valley above. En route, an enormous boulder, the 'Pierre à Gaston', sparks a legendary tale of one Gaston Duseaugey, a wealthy man who reneged on his allegiance to the Devil with the consequence, mild on reflection, that all his gold was turned into stone, this stone.

Once beyond the forest, the path enters a high mountain pasture dotted with cattle, whose milk goes to make the famous cheese, Tomme de Samoëns. These pastures of Folly are among the seven *alpages* ceded to the citizens of Samoëns by Amédée VIII, Duke of Savoy, in 1438, an historic occasion of which the local populace remain rightly proud. The people of Samoëns are known as Septimontains from the seven Alpine pastures, called 'montagne' in the dialect of Savoie

The Refuge de Folly, in times gone by damaged by avalanches, stands atop a rough alpine meadow, rich in flowers: among its varied range of refreshments, the *tartes au citron* are highly commendable.

Pressing on past the refuge, the route comes up against the rock step of Les Eaux Froides, a short barrier of friable slate-grey rock that requires a little care and attention. Attractive green pastures and soaring cliffs lie beyond.

A few more bends, and there, beneath the peak of Pointe Rousse, lies the Lac des Chambres, its rocky flanks and black, gravelly surrounds criss-crossed with pathways, many leading to the water's edge, evidence of it having been frozen in the recent past.

WALK 20 Les Avoudrues (2666m: 8747ft) and Pointe de Bellegarde (2514m: 8248ft)

Grade	A
Ascent:	1820m (5970ft)
Time:	2 days
Start/Finish:	Pont du Pied du Crêt

Map: **IGN 3530 ET: Samoëns–Haut-Giffre**

Very much within the province of experienced mountaineers, the ascent of Les Avoudrues and Pointe de Bellegarde is a superb outing, best accomplished over two days, staying overnight at the Refuge de Folly (Telephone: 50 90 10 91).

An ice-axe, rope and crampons are almost certain all to be needed on this route. The summit ridge provides excellent views across the surrounding mountains and of Les Dent Blanches and Le Grand Mont Ruan.

DAY 1

Use the description in Walk 19 to reach the Refuge de Folly. Once you have left the trees behind, a fine view opens up of the nearby Le Tuet, and back across the vallée de Samoëns to the distant Chaîne des Aravis.

DAY 2

Continue with Walk 19 as far as the Lac des Chambres, passing the lake on the right and heading for the Glacier de Folly. Quite often the whole valley remains covered in snow well into the year, but the glacier lies high on its southern flank, directly beneath Les Avoudrues. Cross the glacier to its far end and from there climb to a brèche in the cliff wall. About 50m from the brèche the first of two short chimneys leads to a second, and so to the airy summit ridge, which you should follow west and up to the summit of Les Avoudrues.

To continue to Pointe de Bellegarde, retreat to the brèche at the end of the glacier, and then descend by the east ridge in the direction of the Col de Bellegarde (fairly obvious, but not named on maps, and lying just west of the summit). From the col, climb easily to the summit.

With care, you may descend from the Col de Bellegarde, crossing steep névé, and retreating to the Lac des Chambres.

WALK 21 Refuge de la Vogealle (1901m: 6237ft) and Le Grand Mont Ruan (3044m: 9987ft)

Grade:	**A**
Ascent:	**2100m (6890ft)**
Time:	**2 days**
Start/Finish:	**Plan des Lacs (Sixt)**
Map:	**IGN 3530 ET: Samoëns–Haut-Giffre**

Not the highest summit reached by walks in this book, but certainly one of the most impressive, and a route very much demanding a high level of mountaineering expertise. The terrain is invariably rugged, airy, exposed crests are encountered, and, to complete the exercise, a glacier crossing followed by the ascent of a steep couloir. Ice-axe, ropes and crampons are essential equipment, and, certainly beyond the Refuge de la Vogealle, only confident and experienced mountaineers should venture. There is very little let-up in the need for concentration and commitment during the second day's walking, particularly towards the end.

The mountain lies at the far end of the long Giffre valley, the final pastures of which, not surprisingly, bear the name 'Le Bout du Monde' ('the End of the World). A two-day ascent is unavoidable, there being far too much work involved for a single-day ascent. Overnight should be booked at the Refuge de la Vogealle (Telephone: 50 90 44 08: one of a small number maintained by the French Alpine Club).

The Refuge, and the lake above it, to the northwest (and easily attainable from the refuge), make a fine Grade B walk in its own right. Allow 3h–3h 30 for the ascent to the refuge, and another 1h to reach the lake, 3h for the descent.

DAY 1

The approach is by way of Samoëns and Sixt-Fer-à-Cheval, along the upper Giffre valley to Plan des Lacs, where there is parking.

From Plan des Lacs head north (signposted: 'Fond de la Combe') into forest, following a wide trail, the Giffre river never far distant, and fed by a number of side streams that have to be crossed. After about a mile, cross the Giffre, and continue between it and the cliffs at the foot of Pointe de Bellegarde (Walk 20). When, a short way further on, the path forks, take the left branch, pass the foot of a waterfall, and continue to a waymarked, steep, airy and well-trodden passage, the Pas de Boret, to surmount a rocky barrier and reach a series of zigzags leading, as you clear the forest edge, to the Chalets du Boret.

The route now heads northwest, climbing a grassy slope, shortly, after a few zigzags, turning southwest to tackle steep rocky bands through which mountain streams have carved shallow ravines. Once beyond this interlude, the direction returns to north, and climbs steep boulder slopes to the foot of a rocky cliff, near which the Refuge de la Vogealle is located.

DAY 2

From the Refuge, climb through a narrow gorge, ignoring a left branch climbing to the Lac de la Vogealle. Cross the stream issuing from the lake, and ascend some steep grassy slopes on the right which lead to a brief level stretch. Aim for a shallow col, near the Tête de Pérua, and then continue, northeast, making a long traverse of steep rocky slopes above quite sizeable cliffs. The objective is the Col de Sageroux, on the Franco-Swiss border.

On reaching the frontier crest, follow it eastwards to the Col des Ottans, just east of the Tête des Ottans. At the Col, leave the ridge and, without gaining height, move south to cross a rocky shoulder projecting from Le Petit Ruan. Once across the shoulder, head, at more or less the same height, to the Glacier du Ruan, which now needs to be crossed, aiming for the base of a wide and clearly visible couloir. Once across the glacier, the couloir needs to be climbed: if it is filled with unstable snow, or looks less than ideal for climbing, use the cliff face on the left (as you look at it).

Above the couloir the route reaches the south ridge of Le Grand Mont Ruan, which provides an airy and exciting finish to the summit. The view that awaits, of the Dents du Midi, the Tour Salière, Valais and the distant Mont Blanc massif, more than amply repays the effort.

Descend by the same route.

WALK 22 Samoëns to Sixt: the Giffre valley (870m: 2854ft)

Grade:	**C/D**
Ascent:	**200m (656ft)**
Time:	**2h–2h 30**
Start/Finish:	**Samoëns**
Map:	**IGN 3530 ET: Samoëns–Haut-Giffre**

Samoëns and the middle reaches of the Giffre valley have largely been ignored in earlier walks en route to higher things. Yet around Samoëns, where the valley is wide and flat, there is much outstanding scenery and fine walking. Much of the route that follows, one of variety and interest, ranging from riverside pathways to very mild scrambling, is shared with the GR5 and the Giffre. The latter is a fine river, in Haute-Savoie second only to the Arve, and calculated to have a flow rate of almost 50 cubic feet per second.

From Samoëns take the road for Sixt-Fer-à-Cheval, forking right just after a roundabout to reach a bridge over the Clévieux stream. Turn right just before the bridge, continuing downstream to another bridge, and crossing there. Near the confluence of the Clévieux and the Giffre the pathway runs along a protective dyke for a short while, until a track can be taken, following the Giffre, at a distance. It is here, as the route moves beyond the purlieu of Samoëns, and the broad basin of the Giffre makes its presence felt, that there comes the first real flavour of the walk, leisurely pursuing for a while the riparian loveliness of the river.

Continue until the track debouches on to the D907 (crossed earlier) not far from the hamlet of Le Perret. In Le Perret turn right crossing the Giffre by a bridge, following a minor backroad leading to Les Faix. Press on through Les Faix to the road-end, which precedes a woodland trail. Shortly, the path slopes down to a meadow, heading back to the river, reaching it at a footbridge not far from the base of the Gorges des Tines, a narrow chasm with steep rock walls on either side, and no apparent way through. This natural gorge was carved out by the tongue of the glacier which gave rise to the Giffre, and is a fascinating place to explore.

To enter the gorge take a path (ignoring the Giffre bridge) on the right, and climbing above two ruined farm buildings back into woodland. This leads to the entrance to the gorge, at the far end of which the steeper sections have been equipped with metal ladders. At the top, the path continues through a jumble of rock outcrops and boulders, eventually to arrive at the foot of a rock wall, passing en route through sparse stands of beech and spruce. Winning a prize for ingenuity, the path tackles the rock wall, aided, at the most awkward section, by another ladder; it is narrow in places, but presents no real difficulties. The view of the whole Sixt basin, from the top, is splendid.

From here another stretch of woodland walking ensues, followed by a gradual descent down a rocky slope, and across a meadow, to reach the Giffre (South), not far from the Pont des Nants. Cross the bridge, heading for the hamlet of Le Fay, and from there either continue to the village of Maison Neuve, or, by minor backroads, head directly to Sixt. This 12th-century town is sometimes known as Sixt l'Abbaye, having had an abbey since its founder, Ponce de Faucigny, constructed one in 1144.

A bus service (enquire at the Samoëns tourist information office before leaving) runs between Sixt and Samoëns for those who need to return speedily. On the other hand, the road from Sixt to Le Perret, and then via Sougey, Vallon d'en Haut and Vallon d'en Bas will achieve the same return in about an hour and a half, using an old variant of the GR5. Vallon d'en Haut boasts some fine old Savoyard houses, and is worth the detour. Equally the outward route can be retraced from Le Perret, for those not impressed by architectural significance.

WALK 23 Lac du Roy (1661m: 5449ft)

Grade:	**D**
Ascent:	**160m (525ft)**

Beside Lac du Roy

Time:	Ascent: 0h 45. Descent: 0h 45
Start/Finish:	Praz de Lys (opposite Restaurant St Jean à Pied)
Map:	IGN Série Bleue 3529 Ouest: Taninges

No more than a simple uphill stroll, the walk to the Lac du Roy, cradled by the Marcelly ridge to the south, provides an easy after lunch excursion, or a perfect excuse for a picnic. If you want some measure of peace and quiet, go early in the day.

At the upper end of Praz de Lys, the Restaurant St Jean à Pied provides the opportunity for lunch. Opposite, there is plenty of room to park cars. Nearby, a path (signposted: 'Lac du Roy', 'La Couennasse', 'Pic du Marcelly') sets off in a businesslike way, but never really fulfils its early promise,

Pointe de Chalune and Roc d'Enfer from Lac du Roy

relaxing its early gradient as it passes through limestone outcrops to reach the wide hollow formed by the encircling summits in which Lac du Roy is found.

Cross the outflow of the lake, and, keeping left, ascend away from the lake on to a low grassy spur from where to survey the surrounding rich-green countryside. Across the plateau of Praz de Lys, the summits of Pointe d'Uble (Walk 14), Roc d'Enfer (Walk 13) and Pointe de Chalune (Walk 12) are most inviting.

WALK 24 Grotte du Jourdy and Pointe de Perret (1941m: 6368ft)

Grade:	**B/C**
Ascent:	**1070m (3510ft)**
Time:	**Ascent: 3h–3h 30. Descent: 2h 30**
Start/Finish:	**Le Jourdy, north of Mieussy**
Map:	**IGN Série Bleue 3529 Ouest: Taninges**

Walkers wanting no more than to ascend Pointe de Perret will find infinitely easier approaches either directly from the Station de Sommant, simply plodding up the west ridge, or by way of the Lac du Roy (see Walk 27). The route described here is considerably more demanding, exposed in places, and visits the Grotte du Jourdy. That it happens to be an entertaining, if slightly contrived, approach that also opens up the possibility of a fine ridge walk is a bonus.

From Le Jourdy join the wide trail extended beyond the parking space to reach a grassy embankment leading up, left, to the forest edge. A narrow path (signposted) leads into the forest, and climbs, quite energetically, following the Stations of the Cross, to the Grotte du Jourdy, a place of religious pilgrimage.

To continue it is necessary to turn a wall of limestone cliffs. A path, marked by green paint, makes an unexpected detour (southeast), before leading back to an enclosed ravine, the other side of which can be climbed with the aid of a number of cabled sections. This passage is slightly exposed in places, but nowhere unduly difficult or intimidating, and leads by a final steep slope to the top of the cliff above the cave. From here a grassy path leads to the téléski de Roche Palud. (NOTE: If you intend returning by the outward route – and if you don't you will need to resolve transport problems – it is important to fix, as you leave it, the location of the return point of entry into the ravine.)

The path wends its way upwards, until finally it reaches the end of a minor road, near the chalets de Roche Palud.

A path much used by *parapente* enthusiasts now runs southeast, and this can be used (crossing ski pistes en route) to reach a grassy ridge near the Chalets du Pertuiset, and from there the long ridge rising to Pointe de Perret.

A short detour (about 1h for the return) will take you to the nearby and higher Pointe de Haut Fleury. These two summits mark the northern end of the long and superb Marcelly ridge, described in Walk 27. Anyone seeking a demanding excursion of the highest order, could do worse than join this walk and Walk 27 at the col (1862m) southeast of the Pointe de Perret. To complete this it becomes necessary to arrange transport from Praz de Lys, or face eight hours of sustained, but immensely enjoyable, walking and scrambling.

WALK 25 Pointe de la Couennasse (1980m: 6496ft)

Grade:	**C**
Ascent:	**485m (1591ft)**
Time:	**Ascent: 1h 30. Descent: 1h**
Start/Finish:	**Praz de Lys (opposite Restaurant St Jean à Pied)**
Map:	**IGN Série Bleue 3529 Ouest: Taninges**

The Pointe de la Couennasse lies midway along the Marcelly ridge and, as part of a more demanding walk, would normally

Pointe de la Couennasse: Marcelly ridge

be included with that. But it is a fine, neat summit in its own right, and worthy of ascent on what would be a short day to keep in form while essentially relaxing between outings of greater demand.

Walk 23 starts this ascent, climbing easily to Lac du Roy (Roi), and continuing along its eastern shore (or ascending the ridge on that side) to gain a broad path near the Chalet du Roy. Follow this broad path until, near an electric fence, it is possible to ascend, right (southwest) on a ridge leading first to Point 1892 and then to the summit. The ridge is not difficult to follow, and becomes a little rocky near the top.

The summit is a fine vantage point, with a most dramatic view of Pointe de Marcelly backed by the far distant summits of the Mont Blanc massif.

Return by the same route, or continue southeast along the Marcelly ridge until, at an outcrop of limestone rocks, it is possible to double back on a path zigzagging down into the great hollow north of Pointe de Marcelly. At Point 1643, a short, steep trail climbs back to the electric fence, near the Chalet du Roy.

WALK 26 Pointe de Marcelly (1999m: 6558ft)

Grade:	**C+**
Ascent:	**505m (1657ft)**
Time:	**Ascent: 1h 30–2h. Descent: 1h–1h 30**
Start/Finish:	**Praz de Lys (opposite Restaurant St Jean à Pied)**
Map:	**IGN Série Bleue 3529 Ouest: Taninges**

Around the ski resort of Praz de Lys there rises a fine ring of summits, Roc d'Enfer and the Pointes de Chalune and Chavasse to the north, and a splendid curving ridge to the south culminating in the shapely Pointe (or Pic) de Marcelly. Marcelly dominates the town of Taninges, at the heart of the Giffre valley, birthplace of the Jacquemards whose ancestors rebelled against the Duke of Savoy in the days before Savoy became part of France. Its fine pyramidal shape, recognisable from many miles away, forms a prominent landmark.

From the parking place opposite the restaurant retreat towards Praz de Lys a little to a minor road (signposted: 'Pic de Marcelly'; 'Le Planey'), and follow this to Brésy, Canevet, and Le Petit Planey before approaching the chalets at Le Grand Planey. A broad track runs on beyond the chalets towards the minor ridge-end peak, Le Planey, a fine viewpoint in spite of its low altitude.

From Le Planey start climbing the ridge, heading north of west, crossing a minor col, and climbing again, now south of west, to start dealing with the main ridge in earnest. The ridge,

The summital cross of Pointe Marcelly

which rises directly to the summit of Pointe de Marcelly, becomes narrower in places, but is nowhere difficult, and is traced by a clear path throughout. Near the top zigzags ease the gradient, which finally relents as you reach the towering cross on the summit.

Best return by the outward route. Just northwest of the summit the main Marcelly ridge sets off for Pointe de Perret and Pointe du Haut Fleury, but can only be gained either by setting off back down the line of ascent to the start of a path contouring across the north face of the mountain, or, by tackling a cabled and steep rocky descent with a fair sense of exposure (see Walk 27).

WALK 27 Pointe de Marcelly ridge (Pointe de Perret: 1941m: 6368ft, Pointe de la Couennasse: 1980m: 6496ft, Pointe de Marcelly: 1999m: 6558ft)

Grade:	**B/C**
Ascent:	**670m (2198ft)**
Time:	**3h–4h**
Start/Finish:	**Praz de Lys (opposite Restaurant St Jean à Pied)**
Map:	**IGN Série Bleue 3529 Ouest: Taninges**

In a region where, for the walker at least, one fine summit succeeds another in endless, but independent, succession, the discovery of a fine, protracted and totally enthralling ridge walk is like finding a pearl in an ocean. In terms of unadulterated pleasure, the ridge culminating in the Pointe de Marcelly is among the finest outings in the French Alps. Sensational positions and vantage points vie with one another, yet nowhere presenting fit and confident walkers with insurmountable difficulties, giving the ridge considerable appeal, only exceeded in this book by the Chaîne du Mont Joly (Walk 64) for sheer entertainment value.

From the vicinity of Praz de Lys, where the walk begins,

there is no indication of the delights in store; Pointe de Marcelly simply stands as a green summit at one end of an equally green ridge. The reality is quite something else.

Begin from the large parking area at the upper end of the Praz de Lys complex, and take the signposted route for the Lac du Roy, described in Walk 23. Cross the outflow of the lake and head for a rising path across the eastern flanks of Pointe de Perret, which, as it approaches the main ridge, swings south-wards. Once on the ridge, a simple ascent leads northwest to Pointe de Perret, which forms an optional start to the ridge, from which you must return.

Set off along the ridge, heading for a minor rise, the Frête de Penaille, the far end of which drops in a short, abrupt rock wall to the continuation of the ridge. Descent of this wall is feasible, but awkward (it is easier in reverse), but can be avoided on its west side by a brief excursion into undergrowth across the top of the immense slopes falling to the Giffre valley below. Just before regaining the ridge, a short passage on a narrow path has some sense of exposure, the slopes here dropping with greater severity, but this hiatus is soon crossed.

Once back on the ridge, which now narrows, a path leads uneventfully through more bushes and shrubbery to Pointe de la Couennasse, from where the final section of the ridge, leading to the enormous cross on the main summit, runs out before you.

The intervening ridge is narrow, and ends with alarming, and even narrower suddenness at the foot of a short rocky gully equipped with cables and metal stanchions. A few awkward moves lead around a small buttress of rock to the start of the gully, which should be ascended making such use of the cable as is felt necessary. From the top of the gully, the summit stands only a few paces away.

Conflict with the rock gully can be avoided by leaving the ridge a little earlier for a path contouring across the north face

Ascending the 'Bad Step' to the top of Pointe Marcelly

of Pointe de Marcelly to join the ridge ascending from Le Planey, but the difficulties of the gully can be exaggerated, and walkers of all ages scamper up and down it with aplomb.

To return you may (a) descend the ridge to Le Planey and retreat down the line of Walk 26, the timed option, (b) use the contouring north face path to rejoin the main ridge until, from the shallow col before Pointe de la Couennasse, a descent is possible northeastwards beneath the ridge rising to Pointe de la Couennasse, or (c) go back down the gully (just a little more awkward than the ascent). How far you then retrace your steps, to the Couennasse col, to Pointe de la Couennasse (Walk 25), or all the way, is a matter of preference.

WALK 28 Tour de Pointe de Chevran (1175m: 3855ft)

Grade:	**C+**
Ascent:	**690m (2264ft)**
Time:	**4h**
Start/Finish:	**Cluses**
Map:	**IGN 3430 ET La Clusaz–Grand-Bornand**

Pointe de Chevran, due east of the town of Cluses, is entirely cloaked in forest, and as such an ideal opportunity to study forest life. Whether this is successful depends on fortune and silent progress. On the other hand, the walk has a pleasing ambiance, best savoured once the initial, and considerable, uphill work is completed. By starting the walk in Cluses, all the climbing is done at the start of the day, but it is equally possible to start from the tiny community of La Corbassière (very limited parking), or from the Croix Verte (plenty of parking) on the Saint-Sigismond–Arâches road. Don't look for a green cross, it's grey!

From the centre of Cluses, take the side road which leads past the Hôtel de Ville (opposite the fountains), and at the end, turn left, continuing to a signposted forest path, roughly opposite the railway station, on the right. Follow this path as it climbs to meet a forest trail. Turn right, and pass through a barrier to begin the serious work of ascending. Stay on the forest trail, following waymarks, until you can leave it, left, to climb into the forest at the start of a long and steep series of zigzags. There is rather an eerie feel about the forest, but it is rich in birdlife and, in season, fungi, the casual study of which will ease the effort of upward progress. In due course, much overgrown and barely noticeable, the ruins at Le May are reached on a small plateau. But do not be lulled into thinking the climbing has finished. Yet more awaits, though the end is in sight, or it would be were it not for the trees.

With some relief, after another set of tight and steep zigzags, the gradient finally relents, and starts easing downwards to a shallow col at the upper end of a long and narrow alpine meadow. From here, with a certain amount of casting about (there is a signpost, but it doesn't help), an indistinct path might be found, heading for the summit of La Dent, from which to view the great rock-climbing cliffs of Maladière. Take great care! – the summit is unfenced, and there is nothing to protect against the sudden drop of almost 700m (2300ft) to the valley below. (Add 0h 45 for the return.)

Returning to the long meadow, set off downwards (at last), passing the chalets at Chevran d'en Haut and d'en Bas, on a fine, striding path that perfectly balances all the effort of the earlier ascent. The descending route arrives eventually at La Croix Verte.

From La Croix Verte, walk, left, along the road for a short distance until you reach a path descending back into forest. This ultimately, and pleasantly, works its way round to La Corbassière, where a signposted path sets off downhill, becoming steeper and more broken underfoot, crossing and recrossing the Englanaz stream, until it reaches the top of the path ascending from Cluses. Follow this back to the town.

72

WALK 29 Le Môle (1863m: 6112ft)

Grade:	**C++**
Ascent:	**1160m (3805ft)**
Time:	**Ascent: 3h 30. Descent: 2h 30**
Start/Finish:	**Les Gallinons (Ayse)**
Map:	**IGN 3429 ET: Bonneville–Cluses**

Standing totally isolated from other mountains, Le Môle has a splendid, 360° panorama over the lower Arve valley, and is worth ascending for that reason alone.

The key to locating the starting point at Les Gallinons is the road between the Mairie and the church in Saint-Jean-de-Tholome, which leads to Bovère. Much climbing (460m: 1510ft) can be saved by continuing around to the parking

Le Môle

space above Bovère, at Chez Béroud, but the lower start, though long and energetic, unwinds pleasantly through forest, and should deter no one.

From Les Gallinons, just after a bend in the road, follow a path setting off into the forest. The route meets a short rocky passage – Le Pertus – and leads to a clearing (ruin near by), from where Chez Béroud is easily reached.

Heading back into forest, and encountering yet more steep ascent on forest trails, the path eventually reaches the chalets of Le Petit Môle, where there is a chalet-buvette, making this an ideal spot to rest before tackling the second part of the ascent.

Once refreshed, take a path on the left, the summit of Le Môle now clearly in view. The path, now clear of the forest, mingles with numerous sheep and cattle tracks, but the general direction, and the final objective, are never in doubt. After a long traverse of the flanks of Le Môle, a final pull is needed up the shoulder of the mountain to reach the summit, surmounted by a cross.

WALK 30 Mont d'Orchez (1347m: 4419ft)

Grade:	C
Ascent:	550m (1804ft)
Time:	Ascent: 2h. Descent: 1h 15
Start/Finish:	Châtillon-sur-Cluses (Prêles)
Map:	IGN Série Bleue 3529 Ouest: Taninges

'Because it is there', is the suggestion given by one local guidebook for climbing Mont d'Orchez, a great wooded island surrounded north and west by the Giffre, and to the south by the Arve. Having many variations on its name – Mont Orchez, Mont d'Orchair, Mont d'Orche – this diminutive summit, unlikely to consume more than half a day of anyone's attention, is a fine, out-of-the-way place to visit, its ascent almost totally within woodland until the last few moments.

The walk, in its lower section unaided by the almost obligatory signposts and waymarking of Alpine walks, begins from the tiny hamlet of Prêles, gained from Châtillon-sur-Cluses by a minor backroad. From the road-end, where there is limited parking, take the track on the right which, working a way around a few enclosures, heads determinedly for the low crest that dominates the hamlet. Higher up a path leads on to the crest, and, after a short traverse across the face of a cliff, continues to the Chapelle de Saint-Innocent, a rustic structure set amid a stand of beech trees, and a site of ancient pilgrimage.

A steepish descent drops to a shallow col (1012m), and tackles the sustained slope on the other side. Further on the path diverts abruptly and unexpectedly, and continues, suddenly waymarked with orange paint, to pass the ancient ruins of the Chalets d'Orchez. Shortly, a brief clearing in the forest canopy affords a fine view of Pointe de Marcelly, across the great gulf of the Giffre valley.

Changing direction again, the path, still shrouded in forest, now makes its ascent of the final summit slopes, aided once more by orange waymarks.

WALK 31 Circuit of Chaîne d'Or (1200m–1300m: 3837ft–4265ft)

Grade:	C
Ascent:	**Virtually none**
Time:	**2h–3h**
Start/Finish:	**Chaîne d'Or**
Map:	**IGN 3429 ET: Bonneville–Cluses**

The great plateau of Plaine Joux is particularly beautiful, a setting of minor knolls and wooded dells, that make this a popular place for walks with young children, invariably, in the case of French families, centred on a picnic. The whole plateau is criss-crossed with pathways from which to devise any number of variants to the suggestion given here, or to abridge it. This is the place for a lazy day.

The village of Chaîne d'Or lies not far from Bogève on the D22, itself a by-road from the main D902, Annemasse–Taninges road. There is parking in the village, and from here descend slightly to cross a riverbed, climbing the other side on a path. Cross the ensuing ridge and descend once more, then, once La Pesse is reached, start heading towards Bouttecul. From Bouttecul another slight descent, east, through woodland leads to an oratory, and on north–northeast to Prés Chevriers, and Chez Béné, beyond which the path turns to the west, to La Tornerie, before heading south to Les Granges des Plaines Joux.

Continue heading south until, at a junction, a path leads west once more to reach the Chalets Sornéi. Pass between the chalets and press on to reach a more prominent track heading to Plaine Joux. Follow this, left, for about 150m, until you can leave it, left, for a forest trail. At a fork, take the right branch, which eventually returns you to the path used on the outward route, not far from La Pesse, where the circle is complete. Only a short journey is now needed to return to Chaîne d'Or.

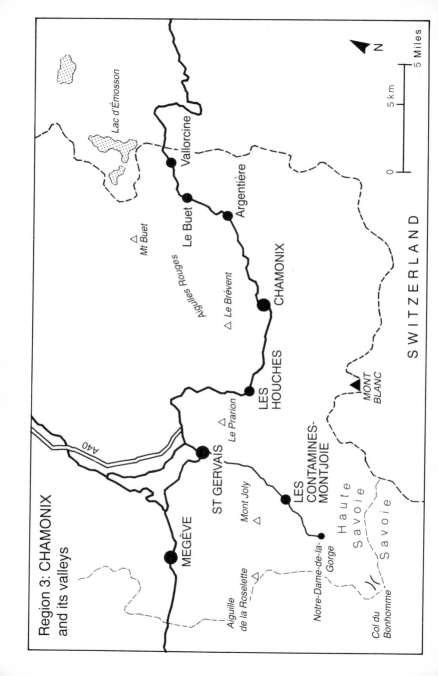

Region 3: CHAMONIX and its valleys

N
5 Miles
5 km
0

SWITZERLAND

Lac d'Émosson

Vallorcine

Argentière

△ Mt Buet

Le Buet

Aiguilles Rouges

△ Le Brévent

CHAMONIX

LES HOUCHES

△ Le Prarion

ST GERVAIS

▲ MONT BLANC

A40

MEGÈVE

Mont Joly △

LES CONTAMINES-MONTJOIE

Haute Savoie

△ Aiguille de la Roselette

Notre-Dame-de-la-Gorge

Col du Bonhomme

Savoie

REGION 3: CHAMONIX and its valleys

WALK 32 Lac d'Émosson (Col du Passet: 1950m: 6398ft)
>   Grade: B/C
>   Ascent: 695m (2280ft)
>   Time: Ascent: 2h 30–3h. Descent: 2h
>   Start/Finish: Vallorcine
>   Map: IGN 3630 OT: Chamonix–Mont-Blanc

Though the lake, and its near neighbour, the Lac du Vieux Émosson, lie wholly in Switzerland, this approach remains entirely within France, just. Whether, on arriving at the lake, you elect to step over into Switzerland to visit the lake or to follow the linking road to the smaller, but in many ways more impressive, lake, is a matter of personal preference; it just seems puerile not to! In any event, there is considerably more to this locality than might at first be supposed.

The walk begins in the small village of Vallorcine, rather dominated by its Gare Internationale. From the station, head for the main road and turn right, leaving it shortly for a campsite (Gîte d'Étape). Once on this backroad, follow it northeastwards, past Le Siseray and the church at Le Clos, and on to the hamlet of Le Mollard, where the road surfacing comes to an end. Passing a few chalets, high above the Eau Noire torrent, and crossing the Nant du Rand by a wooden bridge, the path soon enters forest, and in due course meets a path rising from the tiny community of Barberine (from where an alternative start may be made).

Avalanche-devasted slopes of boulders and fallen trees lead on towards the great Couloir de Barberine, an almost vertical funnel for anything falling from the cliffs above. Before long a splendid and tempting pool heralds the Grand Cascade de Barberine, but since both are affected by unannounced surges of water from the dam above, the temptation to bathe must be resisted.

Rock steps lead on to the base of the cliffs forming the Montagne de Barberine, and out across an impressive corrie basin before climbing energetically, through numerous twists and turns, in and out of sparse woodland, finally to rise beside a small stream to the Col du Passet, with the great expanse of Lac d'Émosson directly ahead, against the backdrop of the shapely peak, Bel Oiseau.

Observant walkers may have noticed (or heard), en route, small red trains ascending the hillside across the Torrent de Barberine. Here a combination of funicular railway, a *train panoramique*, and a small monorail, hoick visitors from the village of Le Châtelard, first to Château d'Eau, and then on to the dam of the great reservoir. The funicular railway was constructed in 1920 to service the building of the dam, which saw completion in 1926. In 1974 it was refurbished to service an entirely different industry, tourism.

Yet there is an even greater secret here, hidden away in the recesses of the Swiss Vallée du Trient. Geologically-minded walkers may well recognise the dark rock formations as being of the type in which fossils can be found, but would anyone expect, at such altitude, to find the fossilised footprints of dinosaurs?

Situated directly beneath the Col des Corbeaux, beyond the southern tip of the Lac du Vieux Émosson, lies an area which more than 200 million years ago formed the marshy frontier between two mighty oceans. Here, today, evidence of the life-forms of that distant epoch remain embedded in the rock for all eternity.

The Lac du Vieux Émosson lies in a vast cradle of rock walls, linked to the larger lake by a broad trail, beyond which a rough path skirts the northern shore of the lake and heads south towards the Col des Corbeaux. It is here, high on scree-and snow-covered slopes, that the fossilised footprints will be found, snow, dust and debris permitting. From the southern point of the lake the ascent is quite strenuous, and a waste of time if snow still lies on the slopes above. Even without this tangible evidence of times gone by, the setting remains awesomely primeval, and more than justifies this brief excursion into Switzerland.

WALK 33 Refuge de la Pierre à Bérard (1924m: 6312ft) and the Col de Salenton (2526m: 8287ft) (Grotte du Buet)

Grade:	**Refuge de la Pierre à Bérard: C**
	Col de Salenton: B
Ascent:	**Refuge de la Pierre à Bérard: 585m (1920ft)**
	Col de Salenton: 1186m (3891 ft)
Time:	**Refuge de la Pierre à Bérnard: Ascent: 2h–**
	2h 30. Descent: 2h
	Col de Salenton: Ascent: 4h–5h. Descent: 3h
	30–4h
Start/Finish:	**Le Buet**
Map:	**IGN 3630 OT: Chamonix–Mont-Blanc**

During the 18th century the Vallon de Bérard was the 'in place' both for Genevois and English naturalists making the obligatory journey to view/study '*les Glacières de Chamonix*'. This high alpine valley, even today, is a spectacular wilderness, a place where the walker encounters a vividly contrasting Alpine landscape of low meadows, around the village of Le Buet, torrential waterfalls, and mature larch plantations. In summer, with glaciated mountainsides cloaked in miniature rhododendron and alpenrose, it is a superb setting. Thankfully, in a region very much kowtowing to the demands of skiers, Bérard has been spared the cables and ironmongery usually found embracing the landscape.

The lazy meandering of the stream that decorates the upper valley belies a dark secret held in its lower reaches, for here it is connected to the Émosson reservoirs to the north, from where

Aiguille de Mesure from the Refuge de la Pierre à Bérard

it receives unannounced and potentially dangerous surges of water.

For most walkers the comparative stroll to the refuge will prove sufficiently satisfying, as indeed it is, while as much time again will be needed for the long but worthwhile pull to the Col de Salenton. Only strong walkers should contemplate the climb to the col. The walk as far as the refuge, not surprisingly, is popular in summer.

33a Refuge de la Pierre à Bérard

Begin at the station car park, near the Hôtel du Buet, by crossing the main road, and following a broad path (signposted: 'Cascade de Bérard' and 'Le Mont Buet') into larch woodland. The path soon reaches a gate, beyond which it leads across a meadow dotted with large boulders. Prominent ahead is the shapely form of the Aiguille de Loriaz, which, with the chalets of La Poya restored in traditional style in the foreground, makes a pleasant start to the walk.

The path passes between the chalets and climbs easily into larch plantations: soon, at a junction, go right. Below, the Bérard torrent bullies a way through a narrow gorge, as the route leads to a bridge by which access is gained to the Chalet-Buvette perched bravely on the opposite bank. Ignore the bridge, and continue on a rocky path above the Eau de Bérard towards the upper valley, which offers agreeable walking.

The first third of the route, on a good path, is a succession of easy ascents and level going, and courts the river, crossing it by the Pont de la Vordette. It leads to a few zigzags, just as the trees are left behind, by-passing a low outcrop, to gain the edge of a large U-shaped valley. In the distance, at the centre of the valley head, the Refuge de la Pierre à Bérard, protected by an enormous boulder, stands out on the landscape, below and to the right of the conspicuous Col du Bérard.

Easy walking ensues, only becoming more demanding as you approach the refuge and cross a small stream; there

A perfect spot for tartes aux myrtilles: beside the Bérard torrent

follows a little to-ing and fro-ing of the path, before it finally tops a rise to reach the refuge. Northwards, Le (Mont) Buet can be seen, over-topping the lip of a large corrie basin, while southeast, the towering cliffs of the Aiguille de Mesure rise starkly against the skyline.

Walkers for whom the journey to the refuge is adequate exercise should simply return by the same route. The refuge has a comprehensive range of meals and drinks, while La Cascade Buvette, down in the valley, serves delightful *tartelette aux myrtilles*.

33b Col de Salenton

The onward route to the Col de Sarenton is signposted from the refuge, and zigzags northwest to tackle a mêlée of tumbled boulders, rock, grass and wild flowers that lead, often across almost permanent snowfields, to even more demanding turmoil before finally approaching the col. Just before the col the ascent for Le Mont Buet (Walk 34) heads northwards, and you should ignore it, keeping left instead, and climbing steeply finally to reach the col.

The col is an impressive location, lying at the edge of the Réserve Naturelle des Aiguilles Rouges, and marks an abrupt and noticeable change in rock formation, where the compact mica-schists of the Alpine orogeny (7–65 million years ago), give way to more friable, darker rock of the earlier Triassic and Lower Jurassic periods (195–225 million years).

Not far beyond the col, and worthy of attention only to those with an interest in geology, lies the Grotte du Buet. To reach it, descend steep boulder slopes on the other side of the col to a wide grassy ledge, and the cave is on the right, a narrow passage between 60 and 80m long and about 4m high. By all accounts it may be safely explored with the aid of a torch and some warm clothing (the interior temperature being around 4–5° C), though, being a little claustrophobic, the author cannot vouch for this.

From the Col de Salenton, the return to Le Buet is unavoidably, but most pleasurably, by the outward route.

WALK 34 Mont Buet (3094m: 10151ft)

Grade:	**A**
Ascent:	**1757m (5764ft)**
Time:	**Ascent: 6h. Descent: 4h**
Start/Finish:	**Le Buet**
Map:	**IGN 3630 Ouest: Chamonix–Mont-Blanc**

Though capable of completion in one long day, as described here, there is much to be said for staying overnight at the Refuge de la Pierre à Bérard (1950m), preferably ascending to it late in the afternoon to enable an early start to be made the next day. (NOTE: The refuge is privately owned, accommodates 30 during summer months only, and provides meals, snacks and drinks. Telephone: 50 54 62 08).

The upper slopes of Mont Buet are almost always covered in snow, making an ice-axe essential; a rope, too, may be found useful beyond the Col de Salenton.

Known to the early explorers as 'Le Mont Blanc des Dames', principally because it was regarded by local guides as a suitable mountain on which to test the stamina and resolve of their clients (male and female) before getting to grips with the 'real thing' across the valley, Mont Buet holds an incomparable position on the edge of the Réserve Naturelle de Sixt-Passy.

The mountain was first climbed by two brothers, Jean-André and Guillaume-Antoine Deluc, noted scientists from Geneva carrying out experiments on the effects of atmospheric pressure on the boiling point of water. They intended, also, to measure exactly the height of Mont Blanc, using a portable barometer. Starting from the village of Sixt, they failed to find a way through the steep flanking valleys of the mountain, and it was to be five years before in 1770 they reached Mont Buet's snowy summit.

These days the ascent is far less frustrating, and begins from the village of Le Buet, from there following Walk 33, first to the Refuge de la Pierre à Bérard, and then on towards the Col de Salenton. The slopes below the col are often covered with snow late into the season, and sometimes all year. Before reaching the col, however, take a trail heading north, crossing a minor spur of the Aiguille de Salenton to reach a prominent platform.

A large boulder here bears the name 'La Table au Chantre', and commemorates Marc-Théodore Bourrit (1739–1819), cantor at the cathedral of Geneva, who, having failed in his attempts to ascend Mont Blanc (though he did reach 4000m in 1784), nevertheless made numerous ascents of Mont Buet.

The Aiguille de Loriaz, at the start of the walk to Mont Buet and the Refuge de la Pierre à Bérard

La Table au Chantre lies just below the ridge separating the valleys of Diosaz and Bérard, and from it the route tackles a rough and trying slope (even more likely to retain snow than those lower down) before reaching the wide Arête de la Mortine, near a shelter (the Château Pictet, 3040m: 9974ft), from where the summit of Mont Buet lies little more than 400m distant.

The summit view is quite outstanding, offering a beautiful panorama of the many Swiss summits, across the massifs of Mont Blanc and the Aiguilles Rouges, and northwards over the vast spread of Chablais.

The descent should be made by the same route. Great care is needed, if snow is present, on the slopes leading from the Arête de la Mortine to La Table au Chantre, and again on the slopes below the Col de Salenton.

On the long approach to Mont Buet

WALK 35 Aiguillette des Posettes (2201m: 7221ft), Tête de Balme (2321m: 7615ft), and the Source of the River Arve (2220m: 7283ft)

Grade:	**B/C**
Ascent:	**1162m (3812ft)**
Time:	**5h–6h**
Start/Finish:	**Montroc (Station)**
Map:	**IGN 3630 Ouest: Chamonix–Mont-Blanc**

Since many of the walks to follow range themselves along the flanks of the Arve valley or its tributaries, it is not inappropriate, given the feasibility and splendour of doing so, to pay a visit to the source of the river, a secluded site, high on the mountain slopes, near the frontier with Switzerland.

The walk begins in the village of Montroc, along a path which runs beside the railway line and bends left where the railway enters the Tunnel de Montroc. Gradually the path moves right and climbs to meet the main road near Tré-le-Champ. Walk along the road in the direction of the Col des Montets for about 300m to a point opposite the parking area for walks to Lac Blanc, and here take another path (signposted: 'Les Posettes') which soon enters forest and starts to tackle the southernmost tip of the ridge descending from the Aiguillette des Posettes. The path continues to rise as it leaves the forest, reaching a left fork, for Les Frettes, gradually working a way up to this fine ridge.

Follow the ridge to the Aiguillette; it becomes more rocky high up, but is nowhere difficult. And it is a fine ridge to walk, one on which it is worth taking a leisurely approach.

Continuing in the same direction, the path comes eventually to the flat Col des Posettes, losing only a small amount of height in the process. To the left of the col, a path descends into Vallorcine, while to the right, its extension heads for the Chalets de Balme. For a short distance, follow the path for the Chalets de Balme, but leave it promptly for another path, heading for the Col de Balme. This, too, is shortly abandoned in favour of a path climbing to Tête de Balme, and the magnificent panorama that awaits. The way is long and all uphill, but the effort is well repaid, for there are few places that offer such an excellent and comprehensive vantage point. A small crucifix stands near by, while far below, the Lac de Catogne has a steely, dark-eyed look about it.

Descend to the Col de Balme, where, just before the refuge, a path will be found traversing the southern slopes of Tête de Balme. This leads to the source of the Arve, close by two ravines.

Return to the Col de Balme, a superb place for lunch, after which locate the start of the Tour du Mont Blanc route, the point at which walkers following that magnificent trail embark on the final stage of their journey. Follow the route down, first to the intermediate station of the Charamillon *télécabine*, from where a service road facilitates a speedy descent to Le Tour, and on to Montroc by road.

WALK 36 Le Grand Balcon Sud (2130m: 6988ft)

Grade:	**C +**
Ascent:	**880m (2885ft)**
Time:	**4h–4h 30**
Start/Finish:	**Argentière, near the Hôtel de la Couronne**
Map:	**IGN 3630 Ouest: Chamonix–Mont-Blanc**

On both flanks of the Chamonix valley a number of walks have been contrived to take full advantage of everything the valley has to offer in terms of views and scenery in general. These 'balcony' walks endeavour to maintain the same height along the valley walls for as long as possible, providing a taste of grandeur without the commitment to scaling greater heights. The two Grands Balcons, Nord and Sud, however, reach heights around the 2200m (7000ft) mark, and involve a fair bit of ascent and descent.

The complete Grand Balcon Sud (described in Walk 41c), which is on the north bank of the Arve, but the southern flank of the craggy Massif des Aiguilles Rouges (hence the South Balcony), is a prolonged walk on a good path throughout: only part of it is tackled here. The gradient is less demanding than might be expected, though the final descent to the Col des Montets is quite steep in places. Even so, it will not trouble regular hill walkers, but places the walk high in its grade.

Not far from the Hôtel de la Couronne in the main street of Argentière, cross a small stream by a plank bridge and climb steadily behind a small building into the forest. Notices here remind you that you are in the Réserve Naturelle des Aiguilles Rouges, while painted stripes on trees and rocks are intended to be helpful, but sometimes confuse. A bend, with a convenient seat near by, a more open section, with splendid views, and a meeting of paths (1437m) follow in quick succession, the latter offering a range of signposted alternatives. A right turn here would hasten you back to the road below the Col des Montets, followed by a simple return to Argentière, but that is not the plan.

Instead, turn left, heading for Les Chéserys, and, passing more tempting seats, climb to another junction (1519m) at which a signpost indicates the way to 'Le Lac Blanc par Les Chéserys'. Follow this to the right. More uphill work ensues, with improving glimpses of Le Brévent ahead before you encounter some of the outlying cliffs of the Aiguilles Rouges. Pass these on the south side, with the path then continuing quickly to the Chalet des Chéserys (1998m).

From a proliferation of signs locate the route for the 'Col des Montets par la Remuaz', and follow this. Regrettably, it climbs even more, but not for much longer. At a large stone cairn the Grand Balcon Sud is finally reached. Before long, at another cairn, the path finally levels out, and continues, now waymarked by cairns, towards the Col des Montets, with the route signposted from time to time.

Eventually, at a signpost, the descent to the Col des Montets begins in earnest. Red arrows painted on rocks guide you through a jumble of rocks and scree, though the col remains visible ahead for much of the way. A building at the col, Le Chalet d'Accueil, is in effect an information centre about the Réserve Naturelle des Aiguilles Rouges. It sells refreshments during the summer season and houses a truly splendid display of wildlife information, including computer programs, slide shows, films, as well as the opportunity to examine curious wriggly things through a microscope.

A simple return down the road to Argentière can now be made, but minor roads, leading to Tré-le-Champ, provide a better, and quieter alternative. Arrival at Argentière is by way of the Chemin du Vieux Four, leading finally to the church.

The Grand Balcon Sud in its entire length is variously described as starting both at La Flégère and Le Brévent. Either way it forms part of the Tour du Mont Blanc, and the ability to solve transportation difficulties from the Col des Montets means that a walk can be undertaken from either La Flégère or Le Brévent (or simply Planpraz), using their respective *téléphériques* to cut out the ascent.

From Le Brévent, take the piste route to Planpraz, and from there head for La Flégère. From La Flégère make for Les Chéserys, and continue the route from there.

WALK 37 Les Petits Balcons (1305m: 4280ft)

Grade:	**D +**
Ascent:	**185m (605ft)**
Time:	**3h–3h 30**
Start/Finish:	**Argentière**
Map:	**IGN 3630 Ouest: Chamonix–Mont-Blanc**

Like their greater and more elevated brethren the Grands Balcons, the Petits Balcons are excellent footpaths along each side of the Chamonix valley, generally maintaining a constant height above the valley floor. This short walk from Argentière is a typically Gallic endeavour to squeeze as much walking as possible into the valley, leaving no potential path untrod, and to present familiar and awe-inspiring views from yet another angle. Gallic logic, too, has seen to it that the Petit Balcon Sud is on the north side of the valley, and vice versa: this round trip uses both balcons, with ample opportunity en route to shorten the walk, and to return, if necessary, from the half-way stage by train (from La Joux).

Start from the car park in Argentière, and turn left into the main street, and then right on to a prominent track immediately before reaching the railway line (signposted: 'Petit Balcon Sud'). Soon the track climbs above the railway line and continues easily through patches of low undergrowth. A more open stretch tackles a downfall of scree and leads to an attractive bridge spanning a tributary of the River Arve. At a junction, continue ahead, ignoring the tracks, left and right, to Le Grassonet and the École d'Escalade.

Soon you reach another junction, and here you leave the Petit Balcon Sud, which ultimately continues to Les Houches, and descend a grassy track across a field for the small village of La Joux (signposted: 'Jonction avec Petit Balcon Nord. Lajoux'). At the approach to the village turn left, following another 'Jonction' sign, to cross the railway at the station in La Joux.

Turn right down a rough roadway, and shortly turn left at a white house on to the Chemin des Cordays. As the river is approached follow the track for Argentière, and continue, invariably following 'Jonction' signs until you cross the river by a wooden bridge. Go left, along the main road for 50m, to locate a path on the right (signposted: 'Jonction avec Petit Balcon Nord').

The route crosses a field to enter mixed woodland, climbing

steeply for a short while to meet the Petit Balcon Nord, there turning left for Argentière. The return to Argentière is delightful walking, and easy underfoot.

Always now the route pursues 'Argentière', rising to its greatest height (1305m: 4281ft), and then gently descending. The route continues to be signposted, either 'Argentière' or 'Petit Balcon', until a wide clearing, La Rosière, is reached. Go ahead here to a large concrete tunnel, cross an unsurfaced road, and continue with the signposting now indicating 'Le Tour'.

Cross the river flowing from the Glacier d'Argentière by a wooden bridge, then keep left and continue following signs for 'Argentière', in due course passing under the railway to reach a metalled roadway. Keep ahead for the centre of the village, through an especially attractive section, finally turning left at the main road to return to the station.

WALK 38 Lac Blanc (2352m: 7716ft)

Grade:	**C**
Ascent:	**475m (1560ft)**
Time:	**1h 30 (Ascent only)**
Start/Finish:	**Téléphérique de la Flégère, Les Praz de Chamonix**
Map:	**IGN 3630 Ouest: Chamonix–Mont-Blanc**

This is a perfect walk for an outing sandwiched between more demanding days. It has enough about it to keep legs and lungs in form, but possesses a relaxing air, fine views, and an excellent high-altitude restaurant at which to while away the afternoon reflecting on past glories and future plans. In good weather, it is quite suitable for young children, providing they are closely supervised.

The village of Les Praz de Chamonix lies only a short way north of Chamonix itself, and from it use the Téléphérique de la Flégère (buy a return ticket) to reach the Hôtel de la Flégère.

The Col du Belvédère: Aiguilles Rouges

Nearby, an orientation table helps to identify the surrounding peaks, of which the Aiguille Verte, above Montenvers and the Mer de Glace, and the Aiguille d'Argentière are particularly outstanding.

At the exit from the *téléphérique* go ahead and descend on a broad track to pass beneath a *téléski*. The track eventually starts to climb, crossing a high mountain pasture (La Chavanne) used for grazing, before reaching a large cairn making the entry to the Réserve Naturelle des Aiguilles Rouges.

The reserve was created in 1974 and comprises large parts of the Chamonix and Vallorcine communes, including the whole of the Aiguilles Rouges massif from the Col des Montets to the Col du Brévent, as well as an important part of the game reserve of Arve-Giffre. This is the first of a series of newly designated 'general' reserves, less strictly regulated than conventional reserves, and will in time extend as far as the shores of Lac Léman (Lake Geneva).

From the cairn a long, more or less level, traverse leads to a short climb to reach a small lake (2171m: 7122ft, often dried up in summer), beyond which more rocky climbing, always on a good path, brings the Lac Blanc and its surroundings into view.

The nearby Refuge du Lac Blanc not only provides accommodation (when the sleeping quarters are not under repair following avalanche damage!); but has an excellent bar-restaurant serving a range of dishes and specialities, from which the *croûte au fromage*, a kind of baked garlicky Welsh Rarebit with an egg on top, is highly recommended – by me, at least.

The lake is splendidly set against a backdrop of high, craggy and genuinely rosy-coloured mountains, the Massif des Aiguilles Rouges, in the middle of which the Col du Belvédère is most prominent, and, in summer, reached by a simple, if tiring, walk into the great amphitheatre below the Aiguille du Belvédère and the Aiguille du Lac Blanc. Across the valley

Refuge du Lac Blanc

the glaciers of Argentière and Tour neatly frame the high peaks, while, from the far side of the lake, in good light and still air, the Mont Blanc massif is mirrored to perfection.

A return by the same route is the usual order of the day, though a rather more demanding option is available. From the refuge locate a path (signposted: 'Lacs de Chéserys') which descends very steeply to the first of the lakes. In the early part of summer, this path is often still covered with snow, obscuring its precise whereabouts, and making an ice-axe (and possibly crampons) essential. A fixed cable aids passage for a short while beyond the first lake.

On reaching a fork, take the path for La Flégère. This is now part of the famed Tour du Mont Blanc and the Grand

Balcon Sud (Walk 36), and continues past the Chalet des Chéserys (1998m: 6555ft), eventually to rejoin the outward route below La Chavanne, from where a simple uphill pull leads back to the Téléphérique de la Flégère.

WALK 39 Lac Cornu (2276m: 7467ft) – Col du Lac Cornu (2414m: 7920ft) and Lacs Noirs (2535m: 8316ft) – Col de la Glière (2461m: 8074ft)

Grade:	C+
Ascent:	Lac Cornu 415m (1361ft), plus 136m (453ft) on return. Lacs Noirs 536m (1758ft)
Time:	Round trip: Lac Cornu: 3h 30
	Round trip: Lacs Noirs: 3h 30
Start/Finish:	Chamonix (Planpraz)
Map:	IGN 3530 ET: Samoëns–Haut-Giffre

A number of permutations are possible here. Strong walkers will have no difficulty visiting both lakes simply by retreating from Lac Cornu to the Col du Lac Cornu and then following Walk 39b. Others pursuing a more relaxed approach may find the walk as far as Col du Lac Cornu sufficient reward in itself, making this an excellent toning walk following or before a strenuous day elsewhere.

Once distanced from Planpraz, the walk assumes a wilder aspect, the route becoming more craggy and bouldery. The gradients, both those crossed and those ascended, are not steep, but in the upper reaches snow often lingers into August, making an ice-axe an indispensable aid. The ease of accessibility afforded by the cable car makes this walk popular, so you will often find slower, less experienced parties ahead.

The round trip involves the use of the Télécabine de Planpraz, located in the Chamonix suburb of La Mollard, and reached by a steep road, Route des Moussoux, diagonally across the square in front of the post office.

39a Lac Cornu At Planpraz walk up past the bar/restaurant

'Altitude 2000' to a spot where a number of routes and pistes diverge. Le Brévent dominates the view to the west, routes to it lying in that direction and, for the Col du Brévent, northwest. To the right, initially north, the combined routes of the Tour du Pays du Mont Blanc and the Tour du Mont Blanc set off beneath a ski tow. Follow this for about 100m, and then branch left on a path across grassy slopes, heading for Col Cornu. Grass gives way to boulders and scree as the path, clear and distinct when free from snow, passes beneath the Aiguille de Charlanon. Beyond, zigzags, rock steps and more scree lead to a small gap between rocks. The steep scree continues as the path makes a rising traverse to a final dose of zigzags leading up to. the Col du Lac Cornu. The lake, frequently frozen and snow-covered, even in summer, lies down a path marked by cairns and paint marks on rocks, itself often covered with snow.

39b Lacs Noirs Follow the above route as far as the Col du Lac Cornu, and, just across the col, locate an indistinct path going right (northeast), climbing slightly, below Aiguille Pourrie, and dropping to the Col de la Glière. The great hollow of the Combe de la Glière to the right is an impressive sight, falling to the cable car station at La Flégère.

A large cairn locates the onward route, rising steadily northwest before heading up a small valley to emerge a little higher than the upper Lac Noir; the lower lake is hidden, a short distance away behind an intervening outcrop.

On the return journey, customarily by the outward route, a variant leads south-southeast from the Col du Lac Cornu, down the flank of the Arête Supérieure de Charlanon, leaving the Arête about half-way down its length to swing sharply north for a short while before crossing the expansive slopes of the Montagne de Charlanon, heading for the ruined Chalet de Charlanon. Near the ruins the descending path meets the Grand Balcon Sud (also the Tour (du Pays) du Mont Blanc) which you can follow, southwest, back to Planpraz. This alternative descent will need a little more time, about half an hour, and, ironically, involves another 185m (605ft) of ascent.

WALK 40 Le Grand Balcon Nord (2233m: 7326ft)

Grade:	**B/C**
Ascent:	**1270m (4165ft)**
Time:	**7 hours**
Start/Finish:	**Chamonix**
Map:	**IGN 3630 Ouest: Chamonix–Mont-Blanc**

If the Grand Balcon Sud provided a grandstand view of the elemental crags and pinnacles, glaciers and snowy ridges that vie to buttress the Mont Blanc massif, then the Grand Balcon Nord places you in the arena of geological conflict, or at least on the very edge of it. This is typical 'middle mountain' terrain, lying above the afforested slopes, but just below the terminal moraines, glacial debris and screes that spill from the Aiguilles de Chamonix. Early in the season snow may still cover the slopes above the forest line, calling for winter walking skills and an ice-axe.

The walk is immensely popular, and unlikely in consequence to offer much in the way of solitude, but its rewards are great, especially if undertaken in its entirety from Chamonix back to Chamonix, the route described here. A less demanding option uses the mechanics of the Montenvers rack-and-pinion railway (the Train Touristique du Montenvers) at one end, and the Téléphérique de l'Aiguille du Midi at the other, leaving you to enjoy the filling without having to eat the crust. By using the railway to Montenvers, the walking time is reduced by two hours, with waiting time (often considerable) and 20 minutes' ascent time to be added back. The same is true at Plan de l'Aiguille, where another two hours can be saved on the descent.

At Montenvers there is a small alpine museum, and the opportunity to descend to and enter the Mer de Glace: all exceedingly touristy, but impossible to avoid in a place as universally popular as Chamonix. And does it matter? – the experience, the alpine air and the breathtaking scenery are reward enough.

The walk begins by the railway level crossing. Cross the main road and head for the Luge d'Été, a summer toboggan run and chair-lift. Keep ahead on a broad stony track (a ski piste) to the right of the toboggan run, soon crossing it and continuing along the edge of trees. Near the Chalet des Planards the path crosses the railway track beyond which a wide woodland trail, constructed in 1968 for forestry work and used in winter by skiers, zigzags upwards offering improving views of the Chamonix valley. For much of its length the modern path replicates one of the oldest in the district, the mountain path from Chamonix, used by crystal hunters who foraged among the mountains alongside the Mer de Glace, notably during the 18th and 19th centuries, bringing down a variety of attractive rock crystals that commanded high prices as decorations on cabinets and vanity boxes.

Not long after the zigzag section ends the path arrives at a junction. Here turn right (signposted: 'Caillet: Montenvers'), soon reaching the Buvette Caillet where snacks and drinks are available during the summer months. Turn left at the buvette and continue zigzagging up through the forest, crossing the railway once more, and pressing on to the top station at Montenvers.

The scene that awaits arrival at Montenvers is superb: not even the hordes of tourists spilling from the trains make an impression on its scale, dominated by the towering needle of the Drus, the Aiguille Verte and the great serpentine ice flow of the Mer de Glace. Looking up the glacier the north face of the Grandes Jorasses is prominent, a towering wall of rock and ice,

Les Grandes Jorasses from Montenvers

and one of the most important mountains in the Alps, while further right and nearer rise the Aiguilles des Grands Charmoz, the northerly end of the Chamonix Aiguilles.

Second only in size to the Aletsch glacier in Switzerland, the Mer de Glace, fed by the snows of Mont Blanc itself, is nature in the raw, a massive, grinding, uncompromising example of the forces that formed the landscape we see today. Every hour the Mer de Glace advances 1cm (about 90m each year), though its overall length diminishes by almost 7m a year. At one time the river flowing beneath the glacier used to excavate an enormous cavern at the snout of the glacier each summer, and inevitably this became a tourist attraction in itself. Between 1590 and 1645, following exceptionally cold winters, the Mer de Glace effectively isolated the Arve valley, a circumstance that prompted some of the populace to have the glacier exorcised – it seems to have worked!

Montenvers ('the mountain facing north', and at one time 'Montanvert' – the 'green hill') is little more than a grassy shoulder above the left bank of the Mer de Glace, and was first visited by outsiders in 1741 when two Englishmen, Windham and Pococke, ventured into the mountains and found a shepherds' hut there. Three years later, Windham wrote an evocative account of his experiences – *An Account of the Glaciers or Ice-Alps of Savoy* – commenting of the Mer de Glace: 'You must imagine your lake [the Lake of Geneva, Lac Léman] put in Agitation by a strong Wind, and frozen all at once; perhaps even that would not produce the same appearance.' In 1779 another Englishman called Blair provided money for another hut – he called it a 'miserable hovel' – that came to be dubbed the Château du Montenvers; it was composed of little more than boulder stone turfed over. A more substantial building was erected in 1795 'to receive the learned men who came there and to contain the instruments necessary for the observation of these rare beauties of nature.' This construction came to be christened the 'Temple of Nature', though it seems to have been principally used by muleteers as an alcoholic staging post, and barely rose above squalid at best. The first inn was built in 1840, and enlarged to an hotel in 1879; the railway came in 1908.

Much of contemporary knowledge of the way glaciers are formed and flow is due to observations made on the Mer de Glace in the 19th century by Scottish geologist James Forbes (1809–1868, Professor of Natural Philosophy at Edinburgh) and John Tyndall (1820–1893, an Irish physicist), who spent long periods in the Temple of Nature.

Before leaving Montenvers a short descent to the Mer de Glace (or a descent in a small *télécabine*) is well worth while.

For a small fee you can walk directly into the heart of the living glacier, where local enterprise each year carves out a grotto; a novel experience.

From close by the museum, and the adjoining Temple de la Nature, start up a well-made path signposted: 'Plan de l'Aiguille par le Signal', soon zigzagging up rocky slopes to reach a minor summit, Signal Forbes (named after James Forbes), and a magnificent viewpoint. A trig point marks the highest spot, 2200m (7218ft).

For a while the onward route descends a little, but then levels and, with many minor undulations, follows a natural shelf, the Grand Balcon. Shortly after the Torrent du Grépon you come to a possible shortcut ('Chamonix par Blaitière') beyond which the path continues finally to reach the edge of a broad hollow, the Plan de l'Aiguille, the highest point on the walk.

By climbing a little, you can reach the nearby *téléphérique* for a speedy descent to the valley.

If following the complete route, press on beneath the cables (though there is another way down close by setting off in the opposite direction) to begin a zigzagging descent to Chamonix that is long, but fairly gently graded and soon enters the shade of forest. Well into the forest you come to a junction. Go right here, and, a kilometre further on, ahead, eventually to descend a little more steeply to the car park of the Téléphérique de l'Aiguille du Midi, across which a tunnel runs to the town centre, conveniently near numerous bars.

WALK 41 Le Brévent (2525m: 8284ft)

Rising above the Chamonix valley with noticeably less challenge than the Mont Blanc massif opposite, Le Brévent is immensely valued not only as a viewpoint, but as a grand mountain walk in its own right. It is, too, a launch pad for the species of humanity that delights in throwing themselves from high mountainsides attached only by string to an insubstantial, but attractively-coloured, patch of nylon in the fond belief that this will prove sufficient to reunite them with family and friends. In the days before the cult of *parapente*, it was hang gliders who practised these dubious antics. The craze continues, dotting the Chamonix skies with bright canopies, and providing light relief for those who prefer feet on something more substantial than thin air.

With the pleasing attribute that it is eminently attainable by the lesser mortals of the alpine mountaineering scene, and by a number of high-quality routes, Le Brévent was first climbed in 1760 by Horace-Bénédict de Saussure, a wealthy scientist of Geneva, who in that year offered a prize for the first person to climb Mont Blanc. It was not claimed for 26 years, and a year later de Saussure himself reached the summit.

Without question, Le Brévent is one of the finest viewpoints over the Mont Blanc massif, distinguished from others by its greater height and fortuitous position.

Three routes, each with varying and unique characteristics, are detailed here. One starts and finishes at the southern end of the Chamonix valley; another leaves and returns to Chamonix itself, making use of a *téléphérique*, Planpraz, while the third provides a grand traverse, using much of the Tour du Mont Blanc and Le Grand Balcon Sud. For all the walks, the general rule of walking in the Alps prevails: make an early start. Into early summer snowbanks may well still linger on the slopes of Le Brévent, making an ice-axe a useful companion.

41a From Merlet

Grade:	C + +
Ascent:	**1005m (3300ft)**
Time:	**7h**
Start/Finish:	**Merlet Mountain Animal Park**
Map:	**IGN 3530 ET: Samoëns–Haut-Giffre**

The mountain animal park at Merlet is reached by a circuitous road, not metalled for its entire length, from Les Houches, a pleasant village, long and narrow, at the foot of the Aiguille du Goûter. At Merlet room will be found to park cars, with difficulty, and refreshments may be obtained, though admission to the park, which contains chamois, bouquetin, marmot and deer in a free-range setting, is not free.

Start up a broad, stony track, and, near the entrance to the park, strike off, right, up a good track, keeping the perimeter fence on the left.

The conifer woodland in this lower section of the walk is well populated with birds, though any thought that a species of humming-bird has been seen, should be turned in the direction of the humming-bird hawk-moth, amazingly similar, but in reality quite different – humming-birds do not exist in the Alps.

Just above the perimeter fence take a narrow track, on the right, signposted 'Bel-lachat', part of the GR5, the Tour du Mont Blanc, and the Sentier du Pays du Mont Blanc; it is waymarked by red and white stripes on rocks and trees. A long, steady uphill pull now ensues, in and out of forest, with incredible views, before you reach and cross the Vouillourds ravine. The ravine involves a little steep, but modest, scrambling aided by metal posts, in a slightly intimidating setting if you suffer from vertigo. Not much further, the path reaches the Cantine de Bel-lachat, a privately-owned refuge/refreshment hut, rebuilt in 1981, the umbrella-ed tables in front of which, and the cool beers from within, must provide one of the most idyllic situations in alpine walking.

Apart from the unavoidable massif of Mont Blanc, the view is of the great Glacier des Bossons, the biggest icefall in Europe. 3,600m (11,810ft) separate top and bottom of the glacier over a distance of 8km (5 miles).

From Bel-lachat, a short uphill section leads on to the long southwest spur of Le Brévent. A delightful scamper follows, keeping to the north side of the spur, with good views of Lac du Brévent and across the Diosaz valley to the distant craggy Rochers des Fiz. Finally the path zigzags upwards to reach the summit, almost certainly overcrowded, the adjacent café offering plentiful, if pricey, refreshments. Walkers carrying their own refreshments will find a measure of solitude among the many rocky hollows below the summit, where with luck the high whistling of marmots will give them away, lurking beneath the jumbled rocks.

From the summit, a return by the same route is the quickest way back to Merlet, though a longer alternative is available. For this, follow the broad ski piste, bearing right and aiming for the Planpraz station below, or simply reverse Walk 41b below. From Planpraz a track zigzags down, across the Combe du Brévent, making for the Petit Balcon Sud, and so signposted. On reaching the Petit Balcon, follow signs for Merlet, keeping to a terraced pathway through splendid woodland.

41b From Chamonix

Grade:	**C**
Ascent:	**525m (1725ft)**
Time:	**Round trip from Planpraz back to Chamonix: 4h 30–5h**
Start:	**Chamonix (Planpraz)**
Finish:	**Chamonix**
Map:	**IGN 3530 ET: Samoëns–Haut-Giffre**

Though significantly assisted by using the Télécabine de Planpraz, the ascent of Le Brévent from Chamonix is in no sense diminished, and is a fine excursion. The cable car station is at La Mollard, up a steep little road behind the church, the Route des Moussoux. Be sure only to buy a one-way ticket if you intend following the whole route.

From Planpraz, where a modern restaurant has replaced the more decrepit structure that existed until the late 1980s, a

Balmat-Paccard statue, Chamonix

choice of routes awaits. The simplest is to follow the broad piste that has been bulldozed across the mountainside, a long and intruding scar without its winter raiment.

A better option makes for the Col du Brévent, waymarked with red and white stripes, gradually ascending northwest from Planpraz until it gains the end of a ridge dropping from the north side of the col. The col is soon reached.

Cross the col and move right for a short distance to enter a hidden valley, curving round behind Le Brévent, before climbing to meet the ski piste once more for the final pull to the summit.

The descent reverses Walk 41a, along the southwest spur of Le Brévent, as far as Bel-lachat. Here, instead of pursuing the track for Merlet/Les Houches, head down for Chamonix in a never-ending series of dusty zigzags alongside which myriad wild flowers, and the view across the valley, ease the descent. The path reaches Chamonix at the Chemin du Belachat, near Les Mollieux, where knees will be grateful for a gentle massage.

41c Col des Montets to Les Houches

Grade:	C + +
Ascent:	1375m (4510ft)
Time:	11 hours
Start:	Col des Montets
Finish:	Les Houches
Maps:	IGN 3630 OT: Chamonix–Mont-Blanc and
	IGN 3530 ET: Samoëns–Haut-Giffre

If two cars are not available to resolve the obvious transport problem, you may use the railway, which passes through a small village, Montroc, not far from Argentière. The walk can begin from Montroc, if necessary, walking up to Col des Montets, adding only a little to time and ascent. If you choose this option, a shortcut, about 450m up the road from Tré-le-Champ, cuts left into the Réserve Naturelle des Aiguilles Rouges (signposted: 'La Flégère', 'Le Lac Blanc'), opposite a sign on the right for Les Posettes. This is a variant of the Tour du Mont Blanc, climbing towards cliffs, eventually to meet the path from the Col des Montets.

Should circumstances counsel their use, there are along the walk a number of escape routes, with cable car descents possible from La Flégère, Planpraz, and Le Brévent. The walk is long and demanding, even more so on a hot day, and it is wiser to reserve the later stages for another day if overcome by fatigue, or a change in the weather.

Leave the Col des Montets by a path near the Chalet d'Accueil, and climb southwest to the meeting point with the path from Tré-le-Champ. Here head west to begin a strenuous climb on seemingly endless zigzags and round rocky knolls to seek out the Grand Balcon, reached at a slanting shoulder known as La Remuaz.

The Grand Balcon now undulates southwest, and, just beyond a right turn (to Lac Blanc via the Chéserys lakes), you reach a large cairn at a path junction. Ascending from the left is the main Tour du Mont Blanc route, having negotiated a delicate moment or two in a rock chimney on the Aiguillette d'Argentière. Continue forward now for La Flégère, visible ahead, but still some time away. The route drops to the Chalet des Chéserys, keeping right, past the building, and ignoring a path on the left that descends to Argentière.

At the Chalet des Chéserys the route reaches the Plan des Aiguilles Rouges, famed for its views of the whole Mont Blanc range. Southeast is the Glacier d'Argentière, to its left the graceful Aiguille d'Argentière with the Aiguille du Chardonnet in front of it; on the right is the Aiguille Verte, beside which the two Drus gaze down on the Mer de Glace.

Easy contouring, more or less, follows along the flank of the

Fallow deer in small numbers inhabit Alpine forests and meadows

Montagne de la Flégère, crossing a number of streams draining from Lac Blanc above. An awkward little corner precedes the drop to La Chavanne, from where a short pull brings the route to the cable car station. Meals, refreshments, accommodation (and an escape route) are all available at La Flégère from June to September.

Continue down a stairway cut in the rock, turning right towards Planpraz, initially through the edge of forest, then crossing pasture and open mountainside. A couple of ruined chalets are encountered en route, at La Glière and Charlanon, before the path rises again, crosses the Montagne de la Parsa, and curves back to reach Planpraz.

You now take Walk 41b, from Planpraz to the summit of Le

Brévent, then Walk 41a in reverse, first to the Cantine de Bel-
lachat, and on, down to the animal park at Merlet.

Continue down the gravel road from Merlet, and after 1km
(about ½ mile) drop on to a waymarked path into forest on
the left heading for the Statue du Christ-Roi. The statue,
erected in the 1930s and dedicated to peace, is the handiwork
of sculptor Serraz. It stands 17m high, set on a 6m high plinth
that houses a small chapel.

The path continues down, leaves the forest and meets the
metalled road near some chalets. Turn left immediately on a
path going straight down, cutting across three bends in the
road. The path comes down to the dam on the River Arve
before another short descent, right, to reach the station in Les
Houches.

WALK 42 L'Aiguillette des Houches (2285m: 7496ft) and Col de Bel Lachat

Grade:	B/C
Ascent:	885m (2903ft)
Time:	6h 30–7h
Start/Finish:	La Flatière
Map:	IGN 3530 ET: Samoëns–Haut Giffre

Of great geological interest, this is a beautiful circuit, but very
demanding: Grade C walkers who want to extend themselves
will find this an ideal testing ground. The Aiguillette des
Houches just manages to raise its head above the afforested
slopes north of Les Houches, and marks a geological transition
from the crystalline rocks that typify the main Alpine summits
to the limestone structure of the Châine des Fiz.

From Les Houches take the road for the Merlet mountain
zoo, but leave it near Le Coupeau to head for the religious
centre of La Flatière. Here follow a wide track (signposted:

'Chalets de Chailloux') heading into pine forest, and remaining there until, just above its upper limit, you reach the chalets. Beyond the chalets the path continues northeast, before swinging to a northwesterly direction and climbing initially across high pastureland and then very steeply in zigzags through boulders and scree to the summit.

The Aiguillette des Houches, a neat vantage point, is the final summit of note along the great ridge wall of the Aiguilles Rouges before it encounters the Gorges de la Diosaz, which effectively separates this fine mountain chain from the summits further west.

Leave the summit, heading north of east, on a path descending below the Pointe de Lapaz and the Aiguillette du Brévent, obscuring the views of the Mont Blanc massif for a while, and crossing a stretch of undulating ground characterised by boggy depressions, streams and small ponds. The objective is the Col de Bel Lachat, though the great rise of Le Brévent dominates the view eastwards; once the col is attained, so Mont Blanc and its entourage returns to view, more than justifying a short descent to the Bellachat Refuge, outside which refreshments and an hour's sojourn are more than welcome. The refuge, however, lies on the line of descent for Chamonix, while the return route to La Flatière demands a short retreat towards the Col de Bel Lachat, before heading into the Ravin des Vouillourds, a short scrambling descent, aided with metal rails, and followed by numerous zigzags and a magnificent descent through pine forest once more, to a meeting of pathways just above Merlet. Here turn right, and contour above the fencing of the animal park for a short distance before descending again to reach a path (signposted: 'Le Lac Noir') heading west for Le Plan de la Cry. Do not follow a subsequent path actually going to the Lac Noir. La Flatière is easily reached from Le Plan de la Cry by a path directly ahead, between houses.

WALK 43 The Bossons Glacier: Chalet du Glacier des Bossons (1410m: 4626ft)

Grade	**C +**
Ascent	**380m (1247ft)**
Time:	**1h–1h 30**
Start/Finish:	**Grange Neuve**
Map:	**IGN 3531 ET: Saint-Gervais-les-Bains– Massif du Mont Blanc**

Walkers who want to climb higher, completing the ascent of the Montagne de la Côte, the line of approach used by Balmat and Paccard during their successful ascent of Mont Blanc in 1786, will experience no difficulty following the well-worn trail up this immense tongue of ground separating the Taconnaz and Bossons glaciers. But the shorter description given here is intended for those who merely want to pursue a (fairly) leisurely walk and inspect the Bossons glacier at close quarters. That the walk terminates at a dramatically-situated chalet serving meals and refreshments is purely coincidental, and nothing whatsoever to do with the predilection the author and his companions came to acquire during the preparation of this book for mid-walk lunches at mountain refuges!

Grange Neuve lies just south of the main Arve valley road, and from here a chair-lift whisks visitors up to see the glacier. There is no doubt that the Bossons glacier is of exceptional interest, rather more than the Mer de Glace, which now reclines a long way back from the thrust of the main valley. By contrast the Bossons glacier almost penetrates to the valley floor, virtually inviting the curious to beat a path to its flanks, which is what has happened.

Over a distance of 8 km (5 miles), some 3600m (11,810ft) separate the top and bottom of the Bossons glacier, much of which falls at an incredibly steep angle, making this the biggest icefall in Europe. The glacier drains the huge mass of ice from the west and north faces of Mont Blanc, and bears silent witness to the many catastrophes that have befallen travellers in the region. In 1978, as Jean-Paul Roudier mentions in the *Dauphiné Libéré*, the tongue of the glacier finally gave up a mailbag from an Indian plane, the *Malabar Princess*, which crashed near the summit of Mont Blanc in late 1950. In 1820, climbers on the Hamel expedition to the summit of Mont Blanc fell to their deaths; their bodies were found 40 years later, at the foot of the glacier. Perhaps surprisingly, since the nearby Mer de Glace is diminishing each year, the Glacier des Bossons appears to be growing again, its tongue having advanced, shifting rocks and demolishing trees, 300m in 30 years.

Walk up from near the bottom chair-lift station in Grange Neuve, traversing grassy slopes to meet the minor road to Le Mont, a small community standing a little above the comings and goings in the valley below. Continue through Le Mont, always keeping roughly in line with the lift cables, and shortly heading left into forest. After a while the path swings right, crosses another grassy section and finishes with the ascent of a piste to the chalet.

From the chalet there is a breathtaking view of the glacier, frequently used as a training ground for would-be alpinists.

WALK 44 Le Prarion (1967m: 6453ft)

Le Prarion is a comparatively minor summit, the highest point of a broad spur of land separating the valleys of Chamonix and Contamines-Montjoie; as a result it can be ascended conveniently from both valleys. Flanked east and west by much lower ground, Le Prarion, on a clear day, is renowned as an outstanding viewpoint.

44a From Les Houches

Grade: C (assuming use is made of the cabin lift to Bellevue)

Ascent:	**181m (594ft)**
Time:	**4h–5h**
Start/Finish:	**Les Houches**
Map:	**IGN 3531 ET: Saint-Gervais-les-Bains–**
	Massif du Mont Blanc

Take the ski-lift from Les Houches to Bellevue, and on arriving at Bellevue follow the signposted route to the Col de Voza, slightly downhill, with the track of the Tramway du Mont Blanc on the left. The path is quite broad and surprisingly pastoral, already revealing its quality as a vantage point. The tramway, a rack-and-pinion system running from Saint-Gervais-Le Fayet to the Nid d'Aigle, was built between 1902 and 1904, and its trains make the ascent of the 25-degree slope in about 50 minutes.

Press on past the Hotel Bellevue and cross the tramway, continuing to follow signs for the 'Col de Voza' and 'Les Houches'. The Col de Voza, when it arrives, is quite a thoroughfare. The tramway has a station here, there is a large hotel, open all the year round, from which refreshments may be obtained, and the col is traversed both by the Tour du Mont Blanc and the GR5, one of the first long-distance footpaths established in France, and extending from the Luxembourg frontier to the Mediterranean. There is a plethora of signs at the col, but one identifies a rising pathway ahead (signposted: 'Le Délevret' and 'Saint-Gervais par Le Prarion'); follow this. The path immediately forks; take the left, higher, branch, climbing steadily to another hotel, the Hôtel du Prarion, visible in the distance. At a junction keep ahead to the hotel. The retrospective view at this point is quite outstanding, dominated by the gleaming white dome of Mont Blanc set behind a contrasting mix of woodland.

From the rear of the Hôtel du Prarion follow signs for 'Col de la Forclaz', with the summit of Le Prarion clearly in view ahead, and later pursuing signs marked 'Tête du Prarion'.

Beyond the Hôtel du Prarion the path lessens in stature, meandering through light woodland and among a scattering of rock outcrops, dotted with small pools.

Near the Hôtel du Prarion a sign, in a masterpiece of understatement, says simply: 'Vue unique'. The view is remarkable, and often elevated to the sublime when the valleys are filled with cloud, through which the encircling mountains project nunatak-like. In spite of its modest height and being overlooked by a 16,000ft mountain, Le Prarion brings its own great sense of elevation, and is an eminently suitable place to linger. To the far east rise the Aiguilles Rouges, and the Aiguille d'Argentière which marks the extreme end of the Chamonix valley, while nearer, the Aiguille du Midi soars above the Bossons and Taconnaz glaciers. Northwest the great fertile plain leading to Sallanches is fully in view, while southwest and south, the heights of the Val Montjoie draw the eye irresistibly.

Walkers returning to Les Houches will find three options available. One, to continue to the Col de la Forclaz and follow a path from there, first to Les Granges des Chavants, then Les Chavants village before reaching Les Houches: this is the most demanding of the possibilities, and is not suitable for anyone ill at ease on steep and sometimes exposed pathways. Less involved is the return to the Col de Voza, using the GR5 and Tour du Mont Blanc route from near the hotel. The path is often excessively muddy after rain or snow, and can be slippery, especially near the top. The simplest return is by the outward route, having acquired a return ticket for the cabin lift.

Anyone not returning to Les Houches might consider the merit in heading down the following ascent from Bionnay, though that, too, involves the initial descent from Le Prarion to the Col de la Forclaz. The descent from the Col de Voza described in Walk 44b may also be used.

44b From Bionnay

Grade:	**C + +**
Ascent:	**1020m (3345ft)**
Time:	**Ascent: 3h 30–4h. Descent: 2h 30–3h**
Start/Finish:	**Bionnay, 3km (2 miles) south of Saint-Gervais-les-Bains**
Map:	**IGN 3531 ET: Saint-Gervais-les-Bains – Massif du Mont Blanc**

Bionnay is a small hamlet just off the road from Saint-Gervais-les-Bains into the Val Montjoie. There is limited parking, and common sense suggests parking somewhere along the main road rather than at Bionnay.

From Bionnay take the Route de Bionnassay, near the chapel, and just after the first hairpin bend go left along a wooded path known as the Chemin du Rocher (signposted: 'Montivon'). The early part of the ascent is through forest and fairly steep until Montivon is reached. Turn left into Montivon, right at a water trough, and left again, on a narrow path (signposted: 'Tramway du Mont Blanc'). A steep pull is needed to cross the tramway, but on reaching a group of chalets at Champlet the gradient relents, and eases downwards to pass beneath electricity pylons. A short way further on, leave the Chemin du Champlet for the Chemin du Plancert (signposted: 'Le Plancert' and 'Le Prarion'). A broad Land-Rover track follows, as far as Le Plan, where you come to electricity cables once more. Continue ahead, up through more woodland, before reaching open pasture. At a hairpin follow a way-marked route for Col de la Forclaz, returning into woodland. Shortly after a small waterfall ignore a turning left, and continue contouring through mature pine woodland until you reach the Col de la Forclaz.

The continuation to Le Prarion is waymarked with red paint, and has been affected in recent years by forestry work. For much of the way it climbs steeply in zigzags through dense woodland to reach the northern extremity of the Prarion ridge. A short exposed stretch has had a cable fixed for security, though the passage is not unduly difficult. With little advance warning, you finally reach the summit trig and the true magnitude of this lowly vantage point is fully appreciated.

The onward route reverses Walk 44a above as far as the Col de Voza, from where, across the tramway, a good Land-Rover track descends to reach a metalled road surface leading to the village of Bionnassay. An easy descent follows to Bionnay, first passing through La Fontaine and making a close acquaintance with the Torrent de Bionnassay, product of the great Glacier de Bionnassay above.

WALK 45 Col du Bonhomme (2329m: 7641ft)

Grade:	**C**
Ascent:	**1119m (3671ft)**
Time:	**Ascent: 3h 30–4h. Descent: 2h 30**
Start/Finish:	**Notre-Dame-de-la-Gorge**
Map:	**IGN 3531 OT: Megève–Col des Aravis**

This is an uncomplicated and deservedly popular walk through the upper reaches of the Val Montjoie to a fine col near the southern limit of Haute-Savoie. Early in the season snow will linger on the approach slopes to the col, making an ice-axe essential.

The river flowing through the valley is the Bon Nant, and much of the land from which it drains forms the Contamines-Montjoie Nature Reserve, in which the landscape, its flora and fauna are given some legislative protection, all the more important in this sequestered corner of the Chamonix region since the walk to the Col du Bonhomme is shared both with the Tour du Mont Blanc and the GR5.

The walk begins from the church of Notre-Dame-de-la-Gorge, built in typically Savoyard baroque style, and a much frequented pilgrimage site at the motorable end of the valley and at the foot of the Gorge de Bon Nant. The chapel contains curious polychromatic statues, and was the former hermitage of Saint Antoine. Not far from the chapel, the Bon Nant is crossed by a wide wooden bridge, giving on to a paved way, of Roman origin, and known as Les Rochassets. This is an ancient through route between Savoie and the Val d'Aosta in Italy, and must have been tramped for thousands of years. The Roman road ascends easily through pine forest and passes a rock arch, the Pont Naturel, off to the right, and worth a moment's diversion.

Cross the river again, by a Roman bridge, the Pont de la Téna, shortly after its confluence with the Tré-la-Tête stream. Continue ahead to a clearing impressively dominated by the Dômes de Miage, the Tré-la-Tête glacier and Mont Tondu to the east, passing among some barns, to reach the beautifully situated Chalet-Hôtel du Nant Borrant.

Continue past the chalet, crossing the Lancher stream by the Pont de Nant Borrant, for a brief while entering the wooded confines of the Bois de la Rollaz, before emerging on a broad track flanked by wide pastureland, passing more chalets, below on the left, La Giettaz (camping permitted) and La Rollaz. The objective, clearly visible ahead below the dramatic cliffs and screes of the Aiguilles de la Pennaz, is the Chalet-Restaurant de la Balme, a very convenient place to halt, take refreshment, or simply give up and enjoy the scenery; it is onward from here that the first of any real effort is required, and La Balme is a marvellously situated disincentive. The view northwest to southwest is dominated by a great frieze of cliffs, extending from the Aiguille de la Roselette (Walk 50), across the Col de la Fenêtre (Walk 49 – through which the Tour du Pays du Mont Blanc passes, leaving the GR5 at this point), to the Aiguilles de la Pennaz.

Beyond La Balme a well-worn track rises southwest (sign-posted: 'Col du Bonhomme'), climbing over rough ground to a

Notre-Dame-de-la-Gorge, Val Montjoie

fork, where the Tour du Pays du Mont Blanc takes its leave, and keeping left to ascend by zigzags to another fork. The left branch heads for the Lacs Jovet (see Walk 46), while the route for the Col du Bonhomme continues ahead, towards an electricity pylon. Before long, you reach a concrete sluice on the Bon Nant, on the edge of the Plan Jovet, the route now heading in a southeasterly direction. When the gradient increases, the path heads in a southwesterly direction, and tackles another steep section to gain the Plan des Dames. En route, on a small plateau, stands a vast tumulus, said to cover the remains of an English woman and her maidservant who lost their lives here during a violent storm. Traditionally, the placing of yet another stone on the mound not only commemorates the tragedy but secures the avoidance of bad luck.

You will come across various paths on the approach to the Col du Bonhomme, depending on the extent of any snow banks, and finally reach the col itself by a steep curve across screes.

The col is a neat saddle, dominated on the east by a double-headed rock known as the Rocher du Bonhomme et de la Bonne Femme, and offering a splendid vantage point. Northwards the view embraces the long line of the Val Montjoie, northeast the Tré-la-Tête massif, south and southwest the valleys of Les Chapieux and the summits of the Beaufortain, and southeast, Tarentaise and Mont Pourri.

WALK 46 Lacs Jovet (2175m: 7136ft and 2194m: 7198ft)

Grade:	C + +
Ascent:	984m (3228ft)
Time:	Ascent: 2h 30–3h. Descent: 2h
Start/Finish:	Notre-Dame-de-la-Gorge
Map:	IGN 3531 ET: Saint-Gervais-les-Bains– Massif du Mont Blanc

One of five walks exploring the upper reaches of the Val

Montjoie, the ascent to the two Lacs Jovet follows a good path throughout, and leads to a magnificent mountain setting. In spite of almost 1000m of ascent, this is unlikely to be found unduly taxing, while the lakeside climax, surrounded by high peaks, is immensely satisfying.

From Notre-Dame-de-la-Gorge follow Walk 45, past the Chalet-Restaurant de la Balme, and as far as the fork just before an electricity pylon. Go left here, ignoring the onward route to the Col du Bonhomme, and soon cross a stream, immediately above some splendid cascades, to gain Plan Jovet. A good path leads on, later dividing a little unclearly. It matters not which path is used to ascend to the lakes, since the alternative provides a perfectly acceptable line of descent.

Upper Val Montjoie

The path which tends rather more to the right is easier as an ascent, and makes for a fine waterfall, beyond which an unexpected level stretch of ground leads to the first of the lakes.

The subtly changing hue of the lake contrasts markedly with the towering snow-clad screes of Mont Tondu to the east and the protective ridge of Monts Jovet to the north. With suitable provisions of bread, cheese and a modicum of wine, an indolent afternoon beside the lake is irresistible (and highly recommended). A short walk around the lake (in either direction) to visit the higher, and smaller, lake, hidden behind a broad rock outcrop, is ample penance for such indulgence.

To begin the descent, cross the outflow of the lake, turn left, and follow a path on the true right bank of the stream, steep and loose in a few places, until the upward route can be rejoined.

WALK 47 Tête Nord des Fours (2756m: 9042ft)

Grade:	B/C
Ascent:	1546m (5072ft)
Time:	Ascent: 6h. Descent: 3h 30–4h
Start/Finish:	Notre-Dame-de-la-Gorge
Map:	IGN 3531 OT: Megève–Col des Aravis

First visited by de Saussure and Pierre Balmat in 1781, the Tête Nord des Fours forms part of the headwall of the Val Montjoie, and is a superb viewpoint for the great summits of the Mont Blanc massif. The walk is quite long and the ascent considerable, so there is advantage in staying overnight at the Refuge du Col de la Croix-du-Bonhomme, from where the climb to the Tête Nord des Fours is possible in a round trip of about two hours. Such an overnight halt would also facilitate the ascent of the Crête des Gittes (Walk 48) within the same day.

From Notre-Dame-de-la-Gorge follow Walk 45 as far as the Col du Bonhomme, and from there head south-southeast on a rough ascending path that soon eases, but is often snow-covered well into the season. After crossing the Nant des Lotharets stream the path heads, more or less level, to a tall cairn on a col. A mapping inaccuracy for a long time gave this col the title, Col de la Croix-du-Bonhomme, while the true Col lies, as the modern IGN maps show, some 500m south of the mountain refuge visible to the south.

Without visiting the refuge, leave the cairn, heading north-east on a variant of the Tour du Mont Blanc, keeping to the left of a ruined house and passing beneath an electricity power line. Easy rocks, also frequently snow-covered, lead first to the Col des Fours, where the variant TMB descends eastwards. From the col press on, roughly northwards for the final pull to the summit on which you will find an orientation table by means of which to identify the vast circle of peaks that stretch as far as the eye can see.

WALK 48 Refuge du Col de la Croix-du-Bonhomme (2433m: 7982ft) and Crête des Gittes (2538m: 8327ft)

Grade:	**B/C**
Ascent:	**Refuge: 1269m (4163ft): Crête des Gittes: 130m (427ft)**
Time:	**Ascent: Refuge: 4h 30 - 5h. Descent: 3h Crête des Gittes: Allow 1h – 1h 15 (round trip)**
Start/Finish:	**Notre-Dame-de-la-Gorge**
Map:	**IGN 3531 OT: Megève–Col des Aravis**

Though following a good path throughout, this walk is long and demanding, and walkers will benefit considerably from an early start. From just below the Col du Bonhomme to the subsequent refuge and along the ridge of the Crête des Gittes snow lingers well into the summer season, making an ice-axe indispensable.

From Notre-Dame-de-la-Gorge follow Walk 45 (Col du

Ascending to the Col du Bonhomme: Chalet de la Balme below

Bonhomme), and Walk 47 (Tête Nord des Fours) for the continuation as far as the tall cairn on the false Col de la Croix-du-Bonhomme. From the cairn a slight rise and easy descent in a southwards direction will bring you to the refuge in about 10 minutes. It is no bad idea to spend a night at the refuge, and then tackle both the Tête Nord des Fours and the Crête des Gittes the next day before descending.

From the refuge head roughly south-southwest to reach the foot of the Crête des Gittes. The onward route, constructed by mountain troops earlier this century, has a narrow, exposed start, and needs great care. After that the exhilaration of the ensuing crest is more than adequate compensation. With snow an ever-present problem here, ice-axe skills are essential, and while the complete traverse of the ridge to Point 2413 is quite outstanding, it is sufficient to terminate the walk at the highest point, Point 2538.

WALK 49 Col de la Fenêtre (2245m: 7365ft)

Grade:	C++
Ascent:	1035m (3396ft)
Time:	Ascent: 3h–3h 30. Descent: 2h
Start/Finish:	Notre-Dame-de-la-Gorge
Map:	IGN 3531 OT: Megève–Col des Aravis

The upper reaches of the Val Montjoie are bounded on the west by a great ridge extending from the Aiguille de la Roselette at the northern end, to the pinnacles of Aiguilles de la Pennaz, considerably higher, at the southern end, though the ridge proper trundles on to finish within sight of the Lac de la Gittaz. A number of high cols punctuate the ridge, but it is the 'window', the Col de la Fenêtre, that offers an acceptable crossing between adjacent valleys, one taken by the Tour du Pays du Mont Blanc. The col lies almost due west of the Chalet-Restaurant de la Balme, from where, at least until the last few minutes, when steep rocks offer a final flourish of

Aiguille de la Roselette (right), and the Col de la Fenêtre

resistance, it may be reached without undue difficulty with a little caution.

Follow Walk 45 from Notre-Dame-de-la-Gorge as far as La Balme, and there take a waymarked track (signposted: 'Col de la Fenêtre'). A number of tracks criss-cross beneath the cliffs, some affected by stonefall, and these in recent years have necessitated slight modifications to former lines of ascent. No such problems should be encountered on the present route.

At the first junction fork right, and press on, rising steadily in a series of zigzags to another junction. Again go right (signposted: 'Les Prés'), following a track as far as a small lake. Here another signpost indicates the way to the Col de la Cicle and the Col de la Fenêtre, taking to a dry valley for progress before reaching open pasture a few zigzags below the Plan de la Fenêtre, a grassy, rock-punctuated alpine pasture, and an ideal spot for a short halt.

The rock walls above conceal the Col de la Fenêtre itself, though the onward route is not in doubt, in places cairned, and heading northwestwards to a final rocky scramble up to the col.

A number of ways down are on offer. The simplest (and the timed route) is to return the way you have come, but by pressing on through the 'window', a short rocky descent leads to a path running north to Col du Joly, and this offers an eminently suitable return to base, making use of the *télécabine* systems that service the col and the winter skiing fraternity.

Once the steep ascent to Aiguille de la Roselette is passed, the ongoing ridge narrows splendidly, but all too briefly, before hastening down to the Chalet-Restaurant at Col du Joly.

From the col a broad piste, one of many alternatives, runs down to the upper station of Le Signal *télécabine*, which will whisk you down to a small, tourist-popular lake, from where the *Télécabine de la Gorge* finally plunges to the valley, about 1km (½ mile) north of Notre-Dame-de-la-Gorge.

WALK 50 Aiguille de la Roselette (2384m: 7821ft)

Grade:	C
Ascent:	515m (1689ft)
Time:	Ascent: 1h 30–2h. Descent: 1h 15
Start/Finish:	Le Signal upper *Télécabine* station
Map:	IGN 3531 OT: Megève–Col des Aravis

Prominent among the ring of summits at the southern end of the Val Montjoie, the Aiguille de (la) Roselette is an easy ascent if the *télécabines* system is used to whisk you high above the valley. Alternatively, walkers who shun these mechanistic trappings of the French Alps can make the long and tiring ascent from Notre-Dame-de-la-Gorge, but the walk described here is aimed at those who want a fairly easy ascent of a prominent summit. To further compound any feelings of indolence, the Chalet-Restaurant du Col du Joly is a formidable barrier to progress, and its balcony a splendid viewpoint from which to survey the landscape of tumbled peaks and ice-carved valleys, or those valiant souls who overcame indolence and set out for the summit. The final ascent to the top of Aiguille de (la) Roselette is quite steep, but short.

A couple of kilometres (1½ miles) south of Les Contamines-Montjoie the Télécabine de la Gorge rises swiftly to meet a higher system operating to Le Signal. Primarily serving a skiing clientele, the télécabines are a useful way of gaining height speedily and easily, and inexpensively (about £6.00 return in 1993).

From Le Signal a broad path (a ski piste) rises gently to the Col du Joly, reached from the west by a motorable, if tortuous, route from Hauteluce in the valley below. There is a good view, too, of the Chaîne du Mont Joly (Walk 64), for those who might want to inspect the ridge before getting to grips with it.

Leave the col on a good path, part of the Tour du Pays du Mont Blanc, heading for the Col de la Fenêtre. When, in due course, this encounters a small rock wall leave the Col de la Fenêtre path, and scramble up the wall, though it is avoidable, with care, on the left. From the top of the rock wall a narrow path cuts a swathe across the top of a grassy ridge, its flanks resplendent in spring and early summer with wild flowers and visiting butterflies. Before long, however, the path begins to rise sharply, twisting and turning in a series of broad zigzags until finally reaching the summit. The panorama of encircling peaks is stunning, making this uncomplicated ascent a worthwhile excursion for a 'rest' day.

Return by the outward route, taking care on the steep, initial descent from the summit, and above the rock wall.

WALK 51 Refuge de Tré la Tête (1970m: 6463ft) and Tête Noire (1974m: 6476ft)

Grade:	**C**
Ascent:	**779m (2555ft)**
Time:	**Ascent: 1h 45. Descent: 1h 15**
Start/Finish:	**Car park, Le Cugnon**
Map:	**IGN 3531 ET: Saint-Gervais-les-Bains–Massif du Mont Blanc**

Perched conveniently to serve alpinists venturing into the icy sanctum of the Tré la Tête glacier, the Hôtel-Restaurant de Tré la Tête is a worthwhile destination in its own right, reached by a twisting trail through sweet-smelling pine forest. The Hôtel-Restaurant is populated by serious mountaineers and casual walkers alike, yet only a little enterprise is needed to find in its vicinity a measure of solitude and peaceful contemplation of the great peaks and rock walls that crowd in from the east and west: Tête Noire, a minor summit only a short distance away, is such a place.

The ascent has a few steepish sections in the forest, and quite a network of pathways, but the way to Tré la Tête is regularly signposted at possible points of doubt.

Le Cugnon is a small, attractive village just south of Les Contamines-Montjoie, reached by a minor road. At the top end of the village there is room to park 30–40 cars (a limited space that soon fills), and from the car park, rising above it, a path ascends steeply into the forest. At the first bend (to the left), another path heads right (signposted: 'Combe Noire'). Follow this, and just after crossing the Nant des Tours stream, start climbing in a long series of zigzags to reach a higher track, where the Tré la Tête is signposted, though the IGN map does not accurately show the footpaths in this section of the forest.

Follow the various signposts for Tré la Tête until offered a choice between taking the Chemin Claudius Bernard (commemorating one of France's noted civil engineers), and con-

On the Tré la Tête trail

---

tinuing on a forest trail. The Chemin is easier and in places spectacular walking, often no more than a broad ledge across the boulder-strewn flanks of the Grande Roche de Tré la Tête, where marmots can often be found at play; the forest trail, equally pleasant, can be used on the descent.

The Chemin, once gained, leads unerringly to the Hôtel-Restaurant, from where a number of paths radiate. One runs southwest, down to the Combe Noire, a good summertime descent, but prone to avalanches early in the season. Another ascends steeply to the snout of the Glacier de Tré la Tête, a rather dusty, rock-strewn, but none the less awe-inspiring situation.

Only a short distance away stands the minor summit, Tête

Noire, much less frequented than the surrounds of the Hôtel-Restaurant, and with a fine view of the upper reaches of the Val Montjoie and the peaks of the Aiguille de la Roselette and Aiguilles de la Pennaz.

Return from the Hôtel-Restaurant by starting back along the Chemin Bernard, but almost immediately dropping left on a stony track, soon to regain the forest, and rejoin the outward route near the Nant des Tours.

WALK 52 Lac d'Armancette (1673m: 5489ft)

Grade:	C+
Ascent:	730m (2395ft)
Time:	**Ascent: 2h 30. Descent: 1h 30**
Start:	**Le Cugnon: 1 km: 0.6 mile south of Les Contamines-Montjoie**
Finish:	**Les Contamines-Montjoie**
Map:	**IGN 3531 ET: Saint-Gervais-les-Bains– Massif du Mont Blanc**

Tucked away below soaring rock walls, and quite unsuspected from below, the Lac d'Armancette invites excellent forest meandering that breaks free from the pines only in the final few minutes. The great summits of the Dômes de Miage are here much too close to be appreciated, other than as a formidable obstacle to upward progress, but this visual limitation is amply compensated by views westwards across the Val Montjoie to the long ridge of Mont Joly. The ascent involves crossing the Combe d'Armancette, a natural chute for anything falling from the encircling cliffs. For this reason, the walk up from Le Cugnon, or at least the upper section of it, is not advisable early in the season when the combe may still be blocked by snow, or after prolonged rain, when the 'stream' draining its upper reaches successfully achieves the status of 'raging torrent'.

The way to the lake is well-signposted, which is helpful here, because there are more paths to contend with than current maps suggest, and those that are on the map are not always accurately represented. Perseverance, however, will bring its rewards.

Begin from the car park in the tiny village of Le Cugnon, ascending briskly to a path junction. Ignore the path going right (this heads for Combe Noire), and swing left to climb in a series of broad sweeps, through a clearing known as Les Plans (keep right at a path junction), and across the Nant des Tours, to another junction just before the Ruisseau de la Grande Combe, near the Maison forestière. Here go left again on a signposted path to recross the Nant des Tours and pass round the minor peak, Mont Freugé, where the awesome spectacle of Combe d'Armancette creeps into view.

The path rises gently towards the combe, keeps right at the first stream, and then swings across the combe on a stony track, and in slightly intimidating circumstances. It then descends to a meeting of pathways, at which the right branch (signposted) leads in a few minutes to the Lac d'Armancette.

The upper section of Combe d'Armancette is prone to stonefall and avalanche, while its stream is often difficult to cross. These conditions are usually encountered early in the season, but are equally problematical in very wet or very dry weather. It is then advisable not to attempt crossing the combe at this height. You should instead descend as you reach the edge of the combe, on a zigzag path that heads quickly down to an easier crossing-point just after the descending path (shown on the IGN map, but not given prominence) encounters one from Les Plans. This alternative brings you, once across the stream, to the original line some way below the Lac d'Armancette, and involves a little reascent. The setting of the lake sanctuary is, however, well worth the effort: a perfect, if popular, place to relax.

The whole ascent may be shortened by taking a variant path

from Les Plans. This heads rather more directly for Lac d'Armancette, and omits the crossing of the combe. It will shorten the time, too, by about an hour. Following this lower alternative would reduce the overall grade to C/D.

The return to Les Contamines-Montjoie is far less troublesome. From the lake set off downhill, crossing a side stream, but not the main combe. Pass the ruined Chalet d'Armancette and continue as far as an oratory, keeping then to a forest trail which will lead ultimately to La Frasse, a minor suburb of Les Contamines-Montjoie, from where a metalled roadway zigzags down to the town. The various zigs are joined by a good path that flows onward through charming modern chalets to meet the main road close by the church.

WALK 53 Col du Tricot (2120m: 6955ft) and Mont Vorassay (2299m: 7543ft)

Grade:	B –
Ascent:	Col du Tricot: 910m (2986ft)
	Mont Vorassay: 1089m (3572ft)
Time:	Round trip: 6h–7h (Add 0h 45 for the ascent and descent of Mont Vorassay)
Start/Finish:	Le Champel (3km: 2 miles south of Saint-Gervais-les-Bains)
Maps:	IGN 3531 ET: Saint-Gervais-les-Bains–Massif du Mont Blanc

The great craggy, ice-embraced, snow-clad summits of the Mont Blanc massif are the province of experienced alpinists, and only rarely allow lesser mortals close enough either to see what they are missing, or confirm their wisdom in giving them a wide berth. Such an exception to this general rule of inaccessibility lies in the ascent to the Col de Tricot immediately below the extended northwestern arm of the Aiguille de Bionnassay and the immense glaciated northwest face of the Dômes de Miage.

The walk begins from the hamlet of Le Champel which lies at the end of a narrow, twisting road from Bionnay in the Val Montjoie. For a short while the route is shared with both the Tour du Mont Blanc and the GR5, and sets off, eastwards, heading for larch forest that cloaks the southern slopes of the gorge carved out by the Torrent de Bionnassay. At a junction keep right (the TMB goes left here), and continue past the Chalets de l'Ormey on a gently ascending trail, alternating forest and pastureland until, just before the Chalets du Chalère it is possible to drop left to cross the Torrent de Bionnassay at the Pont des Places. An alternative track continues ahead past the Chalets du Chalère, ascending steeply in woodland eventually to descend in zigzags into the Combe des Juments. It is debatable whether such a variant is significantly shorter than the route described below; its quality is decidedly inferior, and if time is of the essence, it is better not to start this walk in the first place.

A short distance after the Pont des Places turn right, near a small reservoir, heading east once more, past the Chalets sur les Maures. The next objective is the Chalet de l'Are, reached via steep wooded slopes, from where a path drops steeply to the terminal moraine of the Bionnassay glacier, like all terminal moraines a grey, gritty, rock-strewn place that conveys none of the awesome majesty of these great ice rivers. The glacial river is crossed by a metal footbridge, and leads to a steepish ascent into the splendid Alpine sweep of the Combe des Juments, rich in season with a splendid spread of Alpine flowers. By way of relief from the toil of ascending to the combe, the Aiguille de Bionnassay presents an ever-growing image to the southeast, its soaring ridges and snowy flanks a brutal challenge to all who aspire to these dizzy heights.

Once the lower edge of the combe is reached, a fairly straightforward ascent then continues, past the ruined Chalets de Tricot, casting left and right in broad sweeps, until it finally reaches the Col du Tricot.

The col is a fine point directly beneath Mont Vorassay and a long ridge descending from the Pointe Inférieure at the western end of the Arête de Tricot. The fascination here is undoubtedly the great span of the northwest slopes of the Dômes de Miage, while far below, the pastures of the Miage are a classic example of a glaciated hanging valley, the waters from which still plunge headlong through the Gorges de la Gruvaz en route for the Bon Nant and the Val Montjoie.

Walkers wishing to embrace Mont Vorassay will find the ascent from the Col du Tricot easy enough, returning by the same route. The additional height gained merely enhances the view of the Dômes de Miage and beyond.

It is into the glaciated hollow of Miage that the onward route now lies, speeding down in an endless series of zigzags before reaching the Refuge de Miage. The return to Le Champel, about 3km (2 miles) distant, lies across steep mountainsides and many side streams above the Gorges de la Gruvaz, but is nowhere difficult, indeed by the time you reach the chalets at Les Lanches and Le Tranchet only a gentle downward slope remains.

WALK 54 Chalets de Lachat (1680m: 5512ft)

Grade:	**C**
Ascent:	**590m (1936ft)**
Time:	**3h 30–4h**
Start/Finish:	**Parking space, near Bay, on the road to Le Coudray**
Map:	**IGN 3530 ET: Samoëns–Haut-Giffre**

Visiting the Chalets de Lachat, high on the wooded slopes above Sallanches, is not the main purpose of this walk, they are merely incidental points of reference en route. Much more appealing, and viewed spectacularly from the pathways that visit the Chalets, are the great cliffs of the Aiguille de Varan and the Aiguille Rouge. When viewed with the rays of an afternoon sun spilling over them, the cliffs take on the hue of Dolomite summits, soaring vertically, and a challenge to any red-blooded rock climber. Walks 56 and 57 pay these summits a visit, but walkers wanting a less demanding view of them will find the walk to the Chalets de Lachat, part of the Tour du Pays du Mont Blanc (TPMB), fits the bill perfectly.

The walk begins at a bend in the road (1044m) ascending to Le Coudray, a road-end collection of chalets, reached along a confusing serpentine array of backroads that climb first through Passy and then through the straggling village of Bay (keep following the signs for the Chalet Varan). There is parking space at Le Coudray, but the bend at Point 1044 also provides room to park, and, at the end of the walk, avoids the trek up to Le Coudray.

Heading for Plateau d'Assy

Begin up the road to Le Coudray, and from the parking area take a wide forest trail (signposted: 'Chalet Varan: Zéta: Lachat') ascending northwestwards, zigzagging upwards in broad sweeps to a junction beneath the unseen cliffs of Le Pertuis. Here one path continues to the Chalet de Varan (Walk 55), while a left turn is signposted 'Zéta: Lachat'. Just below this point an overgrown footpath (signposted: 'Sentier Lachat') effects a brief and pointless shortcut: stay on the main forest trail.

Continue from this junction, first to reach the alpine pastures at Zéta, and then, continuing in the same direction (waymarked with the red and yellow flashes of the TPMB) the Chalets Lachat d'en Haut. Stay on the waymarked trail, which has narrowed to a footpath, and descend into forest once more to reach the Chalets Lachat d'en Bas. Just after the first building, at a woodland crossroads, turn left, and continue descending through forest. At another fork, near the Chavan ruins, branch left again, dropping to cross the Reninge ravine. Once across the ravine be sure to follow the path heading for La Tappe, where a metalled road is reached. Follow this down to Hauteville, and, having passed the buildings of this tiny community, turn left, at a bend, to follow a pathway across the Boussaz stream to re-enter Bay. A short uphill walk leads back to the start.

WALK 55 Chalet de Varan (1620m: 5315ft)

Grade:	C
Ascent:	530m (1739ft)
Time:	3h 30–4h
Start/Finish:	Le Coudray, above Bay
Map:	IGN 3530 ET: Samoëns–Haut-Giffre

There are few more dramatic places for lunch than the Chalet de Varan, perched on a ledge high above the Arve valley, and providing a grandstand view of the Mont Blanc massif, the summits of the Val Montjoie and the Chaîne des Aravis.

The ascent to the Chalet is not unduly demanding, and begins from the parking space at the road-end in Le Coudray. From here follow Walk 54, as far as the junction of forest trails at which that walk goes left to Zéta. Here continue ahead (signposted: 'Chalet de Varan') along the Tour du Pays du Mont Blanc (TPMB), climbing in zigzags and eventually leaving the forest below the cliffs of Le Pertuis. Some of the boulders here are balanced in a way that suggests the form of a large chicken, and this has been emphasised by local enterprise and the use of brightly coloured paints: not quite what you would expect in such a dramatic location, but then neither is the wooden man smoking a pipe with a fox on his head that awaits you at the chalet!

Gradually, the path finds its way through the cliffs, giving way to Alpine meadows above, dominated by the pyramid of the Aiguille de Varan. The Chalet de Varan is not immediately obvious, but lies to the right along a level path. It is not the most fashionable of refuges, but it is a convenient staging post (and point of rescue) for anyone tackling the TPMB, and its balcony a splendid place to enjoy a few drinks or lunch.

Just past the refuge a narrow path (still the TPMB) winds down to Curalla, where, once more, it resumes broad trail status, swinging down through the forest (usually signposted: 'd'Assy') until it can be left for a path on the right (signposted: 'Le Coudray'), heading off at a tangent. This continues uneventfully through pleasant woodland, and finally approaches Le Coudray, passing round the first of the chalets on a narrow path (Le Chemin des Discrets). Suddenly, with no warning, it pops out on to the road, only a few strides from the starting point.

At the Chalets de Varan

WALK 56 Aiguille de Varan (Aiguille Grise) (2544m: 8346ft)

Grade	B +
Ascent:	1454m (4770ft)
Time:	Ascent: 4h 30. Descent: 2h 30
Start/Finish:	Le Coudray, above Bay
Map:	IGN 3530 ET: Samoëns–Haut-Giffre

From the wide Alpine pastures that rise to the south from th Arve valley between Sallanches and Saint-Gervais-les-Bain: the great wall of rock to the north, piercing the wooded slope of the Plateau d'Assy, presents a seductive and panorami challenge to walkers. Their ascent is a demanding, but im mensely satisfying, excursion requiring considerable stamin; and the ability to deal with rocky and exposed situations.

Properly, the Aiguilles de Varan, plural, comprise th Aiguille Grise and the Aiguille Rouge (Walk 57), separate(in distance by a mere 400m, but in practice by a gulf almos immeasurable. The first of the summits is more commonl known, in the singular, as the Aiguille de Varan.

The line of least resistance begins at Le Coudray, abov Bay, using a parking area at the start of a forest trail, describe(in Walks 54 and 55, that leads to the Chalet de Varan. Once th level of the chalet is achieved, and just a little before reachin; it, an indistinct, and unnecessary, path threads a way up grass; slopes, through a scattering of boulders, to gain the tip of ; narrow scree run spilling from the cliffs above. To one side o the scree, a path leads to an obvious low point on the skyline that might usefully be christened the Col du Varan. Furthe progress largely depends on one's ability, and the presence o snow, which makes these final slopes and the unavoidabl(chimneys especially dangerous.

Access to the final tower of the Aiguille de Varan is across ; limestone ledge, over which there are irregular and indistinc traces of previous pedestrians (some of them four-footed) making this a test of route-finding.

Cloud-shrouded Aiguilles de Varan

Gradually, the route becomes steeper, passing below a rock wall, and finally, as it approaches the end of the ledge, it reaches the first of two chimneys that are the key to the ascent. Both chimneys present only problems of positioning; neither is exposed, but they need thoughtful and acrobatic placing of hands and feet. From the top of the chimney, continue towards the right to meet a second rock step, fissured by another convenient, and easier, chimney, which gives access to the final section of the ascent, and leads on to the summit across an array of minor rock terraces. This is not easy walking, and can be intimidating, made difficult by a multiplicity of choices that make accurate route description well nigh impossible.

WALK 57 Aiguille Rouge (2636m: 8648ft)

Grade:	**A/B**
Ascent:	**1530m (5020ft)**
Time:	**Ascent: 5h–5h 30. Descent: 3h**
Start/Finish:	**Le Coudray, above Bay**
Map:	**IGN 3530 ET: Samoëns–Haut-Giffre**

The Aiguille Rouge involves a monumental amount of ascent and effort across difficult, confusing and sometimes dangerous terrain. It will prove a slightly more comfortable undertaking if it follows a night at the Chalet de Varan (Telephone: 50 93 61 98) allowing an early start on slopes that would otherwise be tackled in the heat of the afternoon.

From the chalet take the grassy slopes behind that rise to a low point on the skyline, with the conical shape of the Aiguille de Varan (Grise) to the left. At this unnamed col the ascent of the Aiguille de Varan goes left, but ahead will be seen another col separating the two mountains. This is the next objective, but only experienced winter mountaineers should consider crossing to it if the summit slopes are still retaining snow.

Once having reached this intermediate col, pinpoint, along the long ensuing ridge, the slight peak that is the Aiguille

Rouge, located by an oblique ramp rising to a grassy terrace. Having found your objective, go for it, crossing a chaotic jumble of limestone blocks and boulders that can be tricky when wet. Climb a rock step, and so gain a steep grassy slope. Ascend this slope to a narrow gap giving access to the summit tower, composed largely of bare rocks. Turn on the right a vertical rock barrier which rock climbers can climb (but not walkers). This leads to a small platform, then a wider gully, by means of which you surmount another rock barrier. Cross a large rock slab, and climb a final small rock buttress, to approach the summit by easy slopes.

The descent, by the same route, is rather trickier in reverse, and requires a little more care.

WALK 58 Tête du Colonney (2692m: 8832ft)

Grade:	B
Ascent:	1092m (3587ft)
Time:	Ascent: 3h 30. Descent: 2h 30
Start/Finish:	Flaine
Map:	IGN 3530 ET: Samoëns–Haut-Giffre

The highest point of the imposing limestone massif that dominates the mid-section of the Arve valley, Le Colonney gives splendid views of the vertical slab-like walls of the Croix de Fer group of summits, and of more distant ranges, les Aravis, Bargy, Chablais and, unavoidably, Mont Blanc. Comparatively isolated, the whole group of mountains of the Désert de Platé, is frequented by those elusive and temperamental animals, the bouquetins, and, for capable walkers, represents walking country of the highest order.

The ascent of Le Colonney is affected by the retention of snow early in the season, and involves one short section of climbing on the narrow arête of the Col de Tré l'Épaule.

From the *téléphérique* station in Flaine, take the metalled roadway that leads to the old chalets de Michet, and when this forks, take the service road, right, heading towards the Chalets d'Aujon. As the path approaches the top of a *téléski*, leave the track for the Chalets d'Aujon and head southeast, following the line of the Télécabine de l'Aup de Véran as far as the top station.

Due south rises the Tête des Lindars, while all around the limestone landscape consumes what traces of a path there may have been. The route, however, heading for the Col du Colonney, is waymarked with green paint.

At the col, the route goes to the right, and the waymarking changes from green to blue. The ensuing arête leads first to the Tête de Monthieu, becomes narrower as it approaches the Tête des Lindars, and positively knife-edged at the Col de Tré l'Épaule, where a few moments of downhill rock climbing are needed to reach the col.

Beyond the col, the Tête du Colonney rises dramatically, and is climbed by its northern face. The approach to the summit is by a series of fine ridges, rock ledges, and a final short ridge, steep and airy, leads to the top.

The return should be made by the outward route, when the short stretch of rock climbing at the Col de Tré l'Épaule will be a little easier.

WALK 59 Lac de Flaine (1416m: 4646ft)

Grade:	**C +**
Ascent:	**788m (2585ft)**
Time:	**Ascent: 2h 30. Descent: 1h 30**
Start/Finish:	**Luth, small hamlet, reached from La Grangeat**
Map:	**IGN 3530 ET: Samoëns–Haut-Giffre**

Although the Lac de Flaine is easily approachable by road from Flaine, this ascent from the secluded hamlet of Luth is infinitely preferable, and keeps its distance from Flaine itself, with its unsightly clutter of skiing paraphernalia.

From the road-end in Luth, take the forest trail, heading for the Col de la Frête. This climbs fairly steeply as far as the Granges de Luth. Just after the Granges, keep left, and continue climbing steeply, still in forest, to reach the Col de la Frête.

A short, optional diversion here, left, to the Tête de Louis-Philippe leads to the top of an abrupt cliff, which gives a good view of the Croix de Fer range near by.

From the Col de la Frête head east, and, more or less contouring, swing around the broad northwestern base of the Croix de Fer to reach the Vallon de Flaine and the Col du Cou. A short way further on the path branches, and that on the right leads down to the Lac de Flaine. Flaine itself is about 2 km (1.2 miles) east of the lake.

WALK 60 Lac de Pormenaz (1945m: 6381ft) and Pointe Noire (2323m: 7621ft)

Grade:	B/C
Ascent:	Lac de Pormenaz: 964m (3163ft) Pointe Noire: 1342m (4403ft)
Time:	Lac de Pormenaz: Ascent: 3h. Descent: 2h
Time:	Pointe Noire: Ascent: 4h. Descent: 2h 30
Start/Finish:	Servoz (Le Mont)
Map:	IGN 3530 ET: Samoëns–Haut-Giffre

The tiny hill village of Le Mont, above Servoz, like so many of these small, isolated communities, is reached by a twisting road, the D143, both ingenious and confusing all at once. When it finally reaches Le Mont, turn right (signposted: 'Replat de la Fontaine'), and at the first major bend take a minor road leading to a small parking place.

From here head north for a short distance to cross the Souay stream by a bridge. Once across the bridge the path starts heading southeast, on a fascinating track high above the spectacular Gorges de la Diosaz, until it reaches a more level stretch of ground, La Fontaine. Leave the path here, and turn left to begin a demanding climb through forest (signposted: 'Pormenaz'). The general direction is north, but it is a direction scarcely touched upon, so tortuous is the route.

Eventually, heralded by a significant easing of the gradient, and now out of the forest, the path reaches the Chalets de Pormenaz, followed by a virtually horizontal walk of 2km (1.2 miles) to reach the Lac de Pormenaz.

Southeast of the lake, the slopes of Pointe Noire, now seen to be a double-topped summit, make for rather easier going. There are no really prominent pathways, but once you have surpassed a small initial rock barrier, the remaining slopes pose few problems beyond putting one foot in front of the other. You reach the IGN trig pillar (Point 2307) first, and from it the main summit requires a little more care, being along a short and slightly exposed arête.

For the return, from the lake, a shorter option is available. The path southwest of the lake forks not far from the outflow. Take the right branch, and descend into the Souay ravine by a steep path, with one awkward section (that you can pass on the right). The path leads to the Chalets du Souay, from where brief use of the Ayères ski piste takes the route on to a conspicuous path descending left, back through forest, to Le Mont. On reaching the village road, turn left for 300m to rejoin the car.

WALK 61 Col and Lac d'Anterne (2257m: 7405ft and 2061m: 6762ft)

Grade:	B/C
Ascent:	Col d'Anterne: 839m (2753ft)
	Lac d'Anterne: 1035m (3396ft)
Time:	Col d'Anterne: Ascent: 3h. Descent: 2h

Time:	**Lac d'Anterne: Ascent: 3h 30. Descent: 2h 30**
Start/Finish:	**Plateau d'Assy (Plaine-Joux)**
Map:	**IGN 3530 ET: Samoëns–Haut-Giffre**

The whole of the Désert de Platé is renowned for its limestone formations, known colloquially as 'lapiaz' or 'lapies', and, not unlike the limestone pavements of northern England, they provide shelter for a rich diversity of flora and fauna, with the Désert hosting a number of rare and protected flowers, like the *lys martagon* (the Turk's cap lily). With snowfalls heavier than in Britain, the lapiaz of the Alps, however, when covered in snow, pose a real problem to walkers, and there have been a number of accidents, both on the Désert de Platé and else-where. In these conditions, great care is needed when traver-sing what are apparently innocent-looking blankets of snow early in the season.

This walk is in two stages, with the option of retreating from the Col d'Anterne, and of visiting the Lac de Pormenaz. The second part makes the short onward descent to the Lac d'Anterne, and, if time permits, should not be omitted. The walk makes use of stretches of both the Tour du Pays du Mont Blanc (TPMB) and the GR5.

There is ample parking in Plaine-Joux, and the walk begins along the broad track, suitable for off-the-road vehicles but not to others, leading to the Chalet du Châtelet.

At the Chalet du Châtelet branch left to climb to the TPMB, and follow this as it climbs steadily through increasingly bouldery terrain to the hamlet of Ayères-des-Pierrières. Just beyond Ayères, rising beneath the crenellated towers of the Rochers des Fiz, the TPMB continues, ignoring paths left and right, and crossing some difficult terrain, towards the Col d'Anterne, which gradually becomes visible at the far end of the Rochers des Fiz. The Refuge du Col d'Anterne (also known as the Refuge de Moëde-Anterne) lies a short distance off-route, to the east, but can be reached easily enough on the TPMB path, which leaves the route to the Col d'Anterne about 1km (½mile) before the col.

The Col d'Anterne, reached by a final stiff pull, is a broad saddle, marked by a wooden cross, and has a splendid view of the Mont Blanc massif and the Aiguilles Rouges. Close by the two great vertical walls of the Rochers des Fiz, shooting off north and southwest, make the col a natural stronghold, overlooked by the Pointe d'Anterne.

From the col, a straightforward descent leads in about half an hour to the Lac d'Anterne. The lake, lying in a wide mountain hollow, is often frozen over. It lacks any obvious outflow, and its water drains through a fissure in the limestone bedrock.

You can return by the same route, but strong walkers might entertain a diversion to the Lac de Pormenaz (adding little to the overall time), by descending on the GR5/TPMB to the Refuge du Col d'Anterne. From the refuge, follow the line of a long grassy, almost horizontal spine southwards, past the small Lac du Laouchet, followed by a slight reascent before the lake and its central island spring into view. From the lake's outflow a path heads southwest, and when this forks, go right, to descend into the Souay ravine on a steep path, with a short awkward section part of the way down. This route leads to the Chalets du Souay, descending then to Ayères du Milieu, Le Gouet and the Chalet du Châtelet, where it rejoins the outward route.

WALK 62 Lac Vert

Grade:	**C/D**
Ascent:	**185m (607ft)**
Time:	**1h**
Start/Finish:	**Le Mont (La Côte)**
Map:	**IGN 3530 ET: Samoëns–Haut-Giffre**

Inhabited, it is said, by fairies, the banks of Lac Vert early in the morning are a place of quiet contemplation. Any later in the day, and they become a scene of pilgrimage, as motorised visitors, with little distance to walk, besiege this idyllic spot in time for picnic lunches. The walk shuns the obvious approach by car, but endeavours to make of the limited footpath network between the tiny village of Le Mont and the lake something of a gentle outing that will tax no one. That early morning start is essential if you are seeking any kind of solitude, and then it is that the calm reedy waters of the lake take on an iridescent hue, sparked into life by the play of

The constant contrast between craggy summits and Alpine meadows is exemplified here, above Plateau d'Assy

sunlight on golden leaves. Truly an enchanting (enchanted?) place, for a short while at least: aim to be leaving the lake as everyone else is arriving.

The minor road which serves Le Mont continues to La Côte, where the walk begins. The outing can be extended by the simple expedient of leaving the car in Le Mont and walking along the road to La Côte.

From La Côte take the stony track which runs on from the end of the road, and follow this, climbing gently and zigzagging from time to time, until it reaches the delightful glade in which the lake reposes. A path circumnavigates the lake, and proves to be, to the watchful and silent visitor at least, a good way of seeing (or hearing) the forest birdlife: in the main the birds are of the tit family, but there are green woodpeckers and nutcrackers, though these prefer more open ground.

When cars and their querulous occupants start to arrive, so comes the moment to depart, returning by the same route, perhaps to a croissant and coffee in Le Mont or Servoz.

WALK 63 Mont Joly (2525m: 8284ft)

Grade:	B/C
Ascent:	1077m (3533ft)
Time:	3h–3h 30. Descent: 2h
Start/Finish:	Saint-Nicolas-de-Véroce (Plan de la Croix)
Map:	IGN 3531 OT: Megève–Col des Aravis

As part of a walk tackling the fine ridge running southwest from its summit (Walk 64), Mont Joly is an excellent objective, a fitting conclusion to a walk of the highest order. Ascended in its own right, it is no less worthy, and may just prove to be a spur to tackling the whole ridge.

Mont Joly is conspicuous from many directions, and for a long time forms the backdrop for anyone driving towards Sallanches in the Arve valley, from the direction of Cluses, at least until the Dômes de Miage and Mont Blanc muscle in on

Mont Joly

the act. It follows then that the summit is a fine vantage point, and so it proves, in particular providing superb views of the sprawling mass of snow-covered mountains across the valley, and beyond the frontier into the Gran Paradiso range.

The walk from Saint-Nicolas-de-Véroce is not difficult, but it is a sustained climb and in the latter stages involves a strenuous ascent, albeit of an otherwise easy slope.

From the parking space at the Plan de la Croix, take the stony track which climbs to the top station of Télésiège des Chattrix. Here the path forks, and the route takes the left branch, a variant of the Tour du Pays du Mont Blanc, and continues, without rising too much, beneath the Crêtet des Vernes. Just before reaching the Chalets de Porcherey (wooden cross near by), turn right and climb steeply to gain the Crêtet des Vernes amid a gathering of chalets. A wide hollow lies to the southwest, and you should cross this, having first negotiated a rocky outcrop. Once across the hollow, the path reaches the welcome refreshments of the Pavillon du Mont Joly.

The subsequent ascent to the summit is straightforward, but hard work. Behind the pavilion a conspicuous path ascends to Point 2106. You may also reach this point by a more direct, but significantly more demanding line, by sticking to the Crêtet des Vernes. The diversion to the pavilion does, however, invite a respite before tackling the final approach, and has a fine view across the valley beyond Megève to the Chaîne des Aravis.

From Point 2106, continue steeply to a minor top, Mont Géroux, where there is some easing of the gradient, before the final steep pull to the top of Mont Joly. A large cairn marks the highest point, though this has to fight for space with an orientation table and an assortment of solar-powered radio equipment.

WALK 64 Chaîne du Mont Joly (Aiguille Croche 2487m: 8160ft. Tête du Véleray 2452m: 8045ft. Tête de la Combaz 2445m: 8020ft. Mont Joly 2525m: 8284ft. Mont Géroux 2288m: 7505ft)

Grade:	**B**
Ascent:	**1400m (4595ft)**
Time:	**6h–9h (according to the weather; the hotter it is, the longer it takes)**
Start/Finish:	**Le Lait, en route to the Altiport du Mont d'Arbois**
Map:	**IGN 3531 OT: Megève–Col des Aravis**

A quite superb and demanding ridge walk around the entire headwall of the valley southeast of Megève; this is sustained ridge walking throughout, invariably on an obvious path, but one that is friable in places and requires great care. An anticlockwise route is given here, and this is the recommended direction. The whole walk becomes dangerous in rain, because of the nature of the rock, and can be confusing in mist. In good weather conditions, the grade might drop to B/C, but only just: not without reason is one passage adorned with a security cable! Dire warnings aside, this is truly spectacular, with grandstand views of the massifs of Mont Blanc and Beaufortain the whole way. There is no water en route, though the Pavillon du Mont Joly, with its refreshments and shade, becomes an increasingly powerful magnet as the day draws on.

The walk effectively begins at Coté 2000, a pleasant

The 'innocent' start of the Chaîne du Mont Joly

restaurant, and finishes a little further down the valley at Le Lait. Somewhere between the two is the ideal place to leave the car. Finding this inner sanctum from the maze of Megève is not exactly straightforward: aim for Les Choseaux, just before the village taking a hairpin bend for Thelevey and Le Planellet, and continuing from there to the altiport. There is a more direct route out of Megève, but it is far from obvious, and there is little opportunity to park in Megève while you think about it.

In spite of its name, Coté 2000 is not at 2000m (6562ft), but at 1500m (4921ft); it is its link via *téléski* with an otherwise insignificant bump on the headwall slopes that bestows on to it greater prestige than it deserves. Between Le Lait and Coté 2000 the walking is on metalled roadway, flanked by the runway of the Altiport du Mont d'Arbois, into and out of which light aircraft flit on flying lessons, their pilots practising take off and landing with varying degrees of accomplishment.

From Coté 2000 a broad track continues across a stream by the Pont du Nant de Plaine Joux (not named on maps). When a second track branches left, ignore it and continue on a waymarked track ('F1') working gradually upwards, heading west, until, just after passing beneath the Téléski de Rochefort, it arrives at a col, Pré Rosset. Shortly before the end of this ascent there is a short cut up a narrow path (signposted: 'Col de Véry') which climbs left, and intersects the main track descending from Pré Rosset, at a second col, the Pas de Sion. Now the real collar work begins!

Leave the onward and obvious track by locating an indistinct, narrow path ascending from the Pas de Sion into low scrub. Climb steeply on a narrow but clear trod to overlook the upper corrie basin beneath the Aiguille Croche, then continue very steeply, grass giving way to shaly, dusty rock before finally reaching the crest of the ridge at a small cairn, about 200m east of an unnamed summit (2283m: 7490ft).

Looking east, La Chaîne du Mont Joly stretches away to the far-off cone of Mont Joly itself, while much nearer rise the twin peaks of the Aiguille Croche. Due south, the dammed Lac de la Girotte fills a craggy hollow beneath the Rochers des Enclaves, while beyond rises the massif of Beaufortain, and beyond that the Italian peaks of Gran Paradiso.

From the lung-resting comfort of the grassy ridge the onward route holds great appeal, a fine undulating line, that has its beginning in a rather abrupt and immediate descent to a very narrow section of rocky ridge with steep drops on both sides. The going for a while becomes increasingly airy, to arrive at the base of the first of the two Aiguille Croche where a cable has been fixed to aid horizontal and upward progress. Steep and precarious climbing continues to the top of the first aiguille, from where the second and higher summit is more easily attained.

A much less daunting prospect ensues as the route descends northeast then climbs easily to the top of Tête du Véleray. Another slight down and up leads to the Tête de la Combaz, the first of three distinct 'ups' leading to Mont Joly, and one that you can by-pass by a narrow path contouring on the south flank to the next col. More narrow ridge-work follows, though nothing like the earlier section, until the final pull to the summit of Mont Joly, marked by a large cairn, solar panels and a transmitter. A brief halt here once more to take in the by now familiar view is very welcome before the steep descent to Mont Géroux, a minor outlier with no noticeable re-ascent. More downward scurrying leads easily to the Pavillon du Mont Joly and ice cold drinks (hopefully!).

Leave the pavilion, northwest, on a descending track heading for La Croix du Christ and Mont Joux, but take the first left to follow a track to the hillside hamlet of Hermance, from where a waymarked track ('C') leads to Les Blancs. Turn right on reaching a broad trail, for Le Planay, shortly before which

Setting off along the Mont Joly ridge

go left through trees to gain a track, climbing a little and heading right (west) to the farm at Le Petit Lait (Lay). Here direct access to the bridge at Le Petit Lait is barred, necessitating a long, but not unpleasant, sweep northwest to reach the road at Le Lait, from where you can regain your car.

Strong walkers, who can arrange to be delivered to Coté 2000, might consider extending the walk from the Pavillon du Mont Joly, over Mont Joux and Mont d'Arbois, descending from there to Le Planellet.

WALK 65 Col de Véry (1962m: 6437ft) and Mont de Vorès (2067m: 6781ft)

Grade:	C
Ascent	567m (1860ft)
Time:	Ascent: 2h–2h 30. Descent: 2h
Start/Finish:	Coté 2000, beyond the Altiport du Mont d'Arbois
Map:	IGN 3531 OT: Megève–Col des Aravis

A pleasant and uncomplicated walk, exploring on foot pathways that many French people prefer to tackle on mountain bikes (VTT – Vélo Tout Terrain), this trip to the Col de Véry and the Mont de Vorès is not unduly demanding. In spite of the risk of an occasional confrontation with an out-of-control latter-day velocipede, the walk winds through delightful countryside, in the early stages directly beneath the splendid ridge of Mont Joly. Although some uphill work is encountered, in the main the walk is relaxing, and a fine early morning outing.

From Coté 2000 take a broad track across the Pont du Nant de Plaine Joux (not named on maps), and when a second track appears, on the left, ignore it, continuing on a waymarked trail ('F1'), working gradually upwards, until just after passing beneath the Téléski de Rochefort it reaches a col, Pré Rosset. An earlier and narrow path leaving the main trail, and signposted: 'Col de Véry', can be used, but the marginally longer walk round to Pré Rosset poses no hardship, and simply prolongs the pleasant uphill strolling.

From Pré Rosset drop easily to a minor col, the Pas de Sion, then swinging southwest on a broad trail, crossing numerous streams/stream beds beneath the western extremities of the Chaîne du Mont Joly. Finally, the trail arrives at the Col de Véry. Now only a simple walk ensues, westwards, first to the northern summit (2066m: 6778ft), and then southwest to Mont de Vorès.

A fine view awaits, spanning the Montagne d'Outray and upper Beaufortain, the summits of the Chaîne des Aravis, and the distant Mont Blanc massif.

WALK 66 Mont d'Arbois (1833m: 6014ft) and Mont Joux (1958m: 6424ft)

Grade:	C
Ascent:	707m (2320ft)
Time:	3h–4h
Start/Finish:	Le Planellet
Map:	IGN 3531 OT: Megève–Col des Aravis

This popular round of summits, easily accessible from Megève, is unlikely to provide solitude, but its popularity, swollen enormously in winter by the skiing fraternity, is well-deserved, and the scenery of a gentle, pastoral nature (if you can overlook the skiing ironmongery). It is a straightforward walk starting from the busy community of Le Planellet, southeast of Megève, and there is no shortage of chalet-buvettes en route at which to enjoy a meal or other refreshments.

From Le Planellet take the trail, part of the Tour du Pays du Mont Blanc, which ascends steadily to the upper station of the Télécabine du Mont d'Arbois. The route rises gently across attractive Alpine pastures, crosses and recrosses the Arbois

tream, and later joins forces with another path ascending
rom Les Choseaux (an alternative starting point). From the
ki station the summit of Mont d'Arbois, plainly in view to the
outheast, lies 750m and a rise of 30m (*c*. 100ft), distant.

A short descent leads to a minor col, before a rise of some
50m (490ft) across grassy slopes to the summit restaurant on
Mont Joux.

From Mont Joux descend the broad southwest ridge to the
Chalet du Joux, from where a prominent and waymarked path
works its way downwards, for a while in the wooded company
of the Bois d'Hermance, to the chalets at Tornay-Haut and
Tornay-Bas, beyond which it follows the course of the Foge
tream back to Le Planellet.

WALK 67 Crêt du Midi (1890m: 6201ft)

Grade:	**C+**
Ascent:	**880m (2887ft)**
Time:	**Ascent: 2h 30. Descent: 1h 30**
Start/Finish:	**Praz-sur-Arly**
Map:	**IGN 3531 OT: Megève–Col des Ararvis**

In spite of its modest elevation, the Crêt du Midi boasts a
spectacular and comprehensive panorama, embracing not only
the unavoidable massif of Mont Blanc, but the Aiguilles
Rouges, the mountains of Beaufortain and Bauges, the whole
of the Chaîne des Aravis, the Massif de Fiz and the Désert de
Platé. The ascent from Praz-sur-Arly is entirely on the route of
the Tour du Pays du Mont Blanc, and as such is waymarked
(red and yellow stripes) throughout.

From Praz, descend away from the main road to cross the
Arly, and turn right. Shortly, turn left to follow a minor road
to the hamlet of Varins, starting now a gradual ascent that
leads into the Bois de la Grisette. In the forest the trail narrows
and crosses a few clearings, notably at Les Troncs, climbing
steadily to the Refuge du Petit Tetraz. This is served by a road

ascending from the west, which you can use for a short while to swing around to the foot of a broad ridge. Ascend, south and then southeast, to a large cross (1862m: 6109ft), before tackling the final section of the ridge, which is quite steep and slippery, particularly in wet conditions. From the cross, however, another path traverses below the summit, avoiding the awkward section, and doubling back to the summit once the ridge line is rejoined.

The simplest retreat is by the outward route, though there are a few variant possibilities, regaining the Arly valley east or west of Praz, plus a few variants not shown on the map. Virtually all these variant paths are signposted or waymarked; just make sure you know where they lead before using them.

WALK 68 Le Christomet (1852m: 6076ft) and circuit of the Foron valley

Grade:	**C**
Ascent:	**Le Christomet only: 755m (2475ft)**
	Round trip: 850m (2790ft)
Time:	**4h 30–5h (round trip)**
Start/Finish:	**Megève**
Map:	**IGN 3531 OT: Megève–Col des Aravis**

Rising to the northwest of Megève, Le Christomet, and the subsequent circuit of the Foron valley, is a straightforward walk, distinguished by its fine panorama. It is an excellent introduction to walking in the Alps, almost entirely on grass-flanked slopes, but just a little lacking in that true Alpine feel. It is, however, almost entirely surrounded by mountains of a different stature, of which there are outstanding views, and this alone justifies the effort.

Walkers wanting simply to ascend Le Christomet and return by the same route need only begin from the suburb of La Mottaz, but by starting from Megève the whole of the circuit becomes feasible.

Take the N212 out of Megève, heading west, and make for the hamlet of La Mottaz, leaving the main road at a bend. About 200m down the minor road into La Mottaz another road, not immediately obvious, ascends right, between two houses. Follow this road and almost immediately reach an ascending footpath (waymarked: 'Z') that will have heart and lungs in overdrive for a while. Continue with the path throughout its various twists and turns, eventually to reach a barn, and by passing it arrive at a scattered group of buildings that make up Le Mont de la Mottaz.

Go left here, still climbing a little, until the path descends into woodland to cross the Foron stream. Stay with the path until it breaks free of the woodland and Le Mont Platard is reached, all the time following the 'Z' waymark.

Behind the barn at Le Mont Platard another track (way-marked: 'S') sets off up the long ridge leading to the summit of Le Christomet, moving in and out of woodland until it finally reaches the oratory that marks the summit.

The ascent can be tiring in warm weather, but the summit is a most welcome place to rest, from which to take in the spectacular 360° sweep of mountains, a geological à la carte menu from which to select the next course of your Alpine feast. Northwest rises the great Chaîne des Aravis, moving eastwards to the Petit and Grand Croise Baulet, the distant craggy top of Pointe Percée, the Aiguilles de Warens (Varan), and south to the Chaîne du Mont Joly and the Massif de Véry. Far to the east the dazzling snow-capped summits of the Mont Blanc massif constantly draw the eye, an ever present and formidable boundary to the walks contained in this book.

Walkers returning to La Mottaz should now simply retrace their steps; otherwise, by moving from the summit anti-clock-wise around a ski-lift building you will locate a broad path (waymarked: 'S') descending northwards to a minor top, L'Éperon (1778m: 5835ft), and from there continue to the next hillock (unnamed) from where you can descend northwards to the Col de Jaillet.

The whole of this elevated section is flanked by low shrubs among which bilberries are prominent (and very tasty): many Alpine flowers grow here, too, notably the yellow gentian (*Gentiana lucea*).

From the Col de Jaillet a broad path (waymarked: 'P') heads east towards the Sommet des Salles, but before reaching the summit, at 1687, go right on a forest trail (signposted: 'Croix des Salles') that roughly contours beneath the summit to begin the descent to the Chalet-Hôtel du Jaillet, where refreshments could well delay the onward descent for a while.

Continue descending (waymarked: 'P') on a track which, since the spot height west of the Sommet des Salles, is part of the splendid Tour du Pays du Mont Blanc, crossing two minor roads finally to reach the suburb of Megève known as Le Coin, from where you can easily reach the town centre.

WALK 69 Le Petit and Le Grand Croise Baulet (2009m: 6590ft and 2296m: 7530ft)

Grade:	B/C
Ascent:	Le Petit Croise Baulet only: 460m (1510ft)
	Round trip: 905m (2970ft)
Time:	4h–5h (both summits)
Start/Finish:	Les Frasses car park at the head of the Foron valley
Map:	IGN 3531 OT: Megève–Col des Aravis, or
	IGN 3430 ET: La Clusaz – Grand-Bornand

Strong walkers looking for a long day should have no difficulty adding both these mountains to Walk 68, a commendable prospect, scampering out to the mountains from the Col de Jaillet, that would be enhanced by an early start in the cool of the morning. Those with less demanding aspirations

Croise-Baulet from Le Christomet

can save a lot of initial effort by driving to the car park at Les Frasses, following a rather circuitous route from Le Coin, a suburb of Megève, and making for the hamlets of Allard and Le Mont de la Mottaz before heading straight up the valley. (NOTE: The road to Les Frasses is not on map 3430 ET.)

From Les Frasses car park follow a prominent route (waymarked: 'X') to the Chalet des Frasses, continuing through woodland to a col west of the Sommet des Salles (the Plan des Crêtes – not named on maps), and from there contouring on a broad path (waymarked: 'P') to the Col de Jaillet on which there is a Roman stone marker bearing the initials F I N E S (about which I have been able to discover nothing). Once the Plan des Crêtes is reached the onward path forms part of that classic walk, the Tour du Pays du Mont Blanc.

Viewed from the Col de Jaillet the summits, Le Petit rather more than Le Grand (which is partly obscured) seem to offer little more than a heart-rending slog up grassy or wooded slopes, but this is greatly eased by ever improving views and the comfort of a good path. Take care leaving the Col de Jaillet not to wander off along the wrong path; of the two paths that confront you take that on the right, heading northwest through a spruce plantation, finally breaking free of it below the first summit.

A steady descent northwards leads uneventfully from Le Petit Croise Baulet to the Col de l'Avenaz from where open slopes head up the final arête to the summit. The Tour du Pays du Mont Blanc abandons the ascent just below the last part.

A breathtaking view attends arrival at the summit, of towering mountains and deeply cleft valleys, one that is all the more satisfying for being hidden, partly at least, for most of the ascent. West across the Arrondine valley and north over the Val de Coeur, rise the mountains that comprise the Chaîne des Aravis, great craggy peaks that excite and invite, while to the east the snow-capped heights of the Mont Blanc massif lie along the distant horizon.

A return by the same route is advised, though by continuing due south from the Col de Jaillet, heading for Le Christomet on a path waymarked 'S1', it is possible to return to Les Frasses from the col below the minor top, L'Éperon. This soon heads into woodland, and is boggy in places.

WALK 70 Tête du Torraz (1930m: 6332ft)

Grade:	C+
Ascent:	780m (2559ft)
Time:	6h–6h 30

Start/Finish: **La Touvière, between Flumet and Praz-sur-Arly, and southeast of the Signal du Sac**

Map: **IGN 3531 OT: Megève–Col des Aravis**

Rising to the west of Le Christomet (Walk 68), and with a little more height, the Tête du Torraz is, like Le Christomet, a popular family walk, though the ascent is considerable for very young children. The view from the summit is much the same as from Le Christomet, though it lies rather closer to the Col des Aravis, the Aiguille de Borderan and the Pointe des Verres in particular, and overlooks the busy town of La Giettaz.

Walkers with a taste for wild raspberries and bilberries will find, from about mid-August onwards, considerable excuse for delay: at these times, a couple of plastic containers may prove useful additions to one's day sac.

At La Touvière, the motorable road deteriorates to one more suited to four-wheel drive and off-the-road vehicles, and progress beyond this point is not recommended for normal vehicles. The track continues to, and beyond, Sciozier, which makes a suitable starting and finishing point: anyone able to drive to Sciozier will save 30–40 minutes overall.

From Sciozier, continue along the track, ignoring the branch on the right to La Bonne Fontaine, by which route we will return, and head left instead (signposted: 'Le Gateau') to reach an orientation table on a broad ridge descending from the Signal du Sac.

Set off northeastwards along a forest trail (signposted: 'Tête du Torraz'), and at another fork, again keep left, following an undulating, wooded ridge, now in a northwesterly direction. Once it has left the woodland, the path moves on to the ridge, and swings round to the northeast once more to make its final approach to the summit.

Continue east from the summit until, just after the Tête du Petit Torraz, it becomes possible to descend to the Gîte d'Étape at the Plan de l'Aar. Here the route has joined the

Tour du Pays du Mont Blanc, and you follow this (waymarked red and yellow) to a fork, near the base of a wooded ridge. Take the right branch and head for La Bonne Fontaine. A few hundred metres beyond La Bonne Fontaine, at another junction, take the left branch. This returns you directly to Sciozier, and the road down to La Touvière.

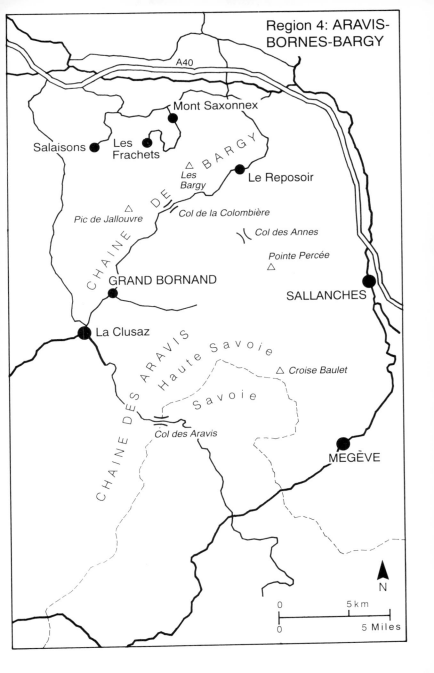

Region 4: ARAVIS-BORNES-BARGY

Mont Saxonnex

Salaisons   Les Frachets

CHAINE DE BARGY

Les Bargy

Le Reposoir

Pic de Jallouvre

Col de la Colombière

Col des Annes

Pointe Percée

GRAND BORNAND

SALLANCHES

La Clusaz

CHAINE DES ARAVIS   Haute Savoie

Croise Baulet

Savoie

Col des Aravis

MEGÈVE

A40

N

0   5 km

0   5 Miles

REGION 4: ARAVIS–BORNES–BARGY

WALK 71 Les Quatre-Têtes (2364m: 7756ft)

Grade:	**B+**
Ascent:	**1548m (5079ft)**
Time:	**Ascent: 4h 30. Descent: 3h**
Start/Finish:	**Plan Chevalier, between Burzier and Outredière (Parking)**
Map:	**3430 ET: La Clusaz–Grand-Bornand**

Les Quatre-Têtes displays its 'four heads' to best advantage to anyone perched on the hillside between Combloux and Saint-Gervais-les-Bains, and though overshadowed by the rocky spire of Pointe Percée, it is nevertheless an inviting summit, and, with more than 1500m (5000ft) of ascent to contend with, a demanding undertaking.

The route given here uses a footpath renovated in recent years, which is considerably better than the boring access trail from Burzier. As a result, it is not clearly marked on the maps, though sections of it are shown. A few short passages above the ravines of the Torrent de Dière require care, particularly after rain, but there is nothing about any part of the walk to pose extreme problems for strong walkers.

From Plan Chevalier continue along the road as far as Outredière, and at the end of the road, turn right. A path, signposted 'Pierre à Voix', leaves at this point, crossing meadows. Ignore this, and turn immediately to the left on a path running alongside a hedge. A steep pull ensues, after which another path is encountered, this time heading more or less horizontally to Pierre à Voix (a strange standing stone in the middle of the forest). Once again, ignore this diversion, and begin an energetic pull, through the forest and across a number of clearings, zigzagging upwards to reach a much-ravined section about level with the unseen Cascade de Doran. The route deals with a few rocky outcrops and buttresses by

The northern end of the Chaîne des Aravis. Pointe Percée is at the left, then Les Quatre Têtes. The Col de la Forclaz is at the right.

passing them on the left, and continues a long traverse across a number of gullies, slippery when wet.

Eventually, the path reaches a small waterworks building (Station de captage des eaux de Sallanches). Shortly, it crosses the mountain stream by a footbridge, and, at a fork, takes the right branch. Before long you leave this branch for a steep winding footpath that climbs to the lip of the wide hanging valley of Doran, soon reaching the splendidly situated Refuge de Doran. An overnight halt at the refuge (Telephone: 50 58 08 00), following an afternoon ascent from Outredière, will allow the 2½–3 hours of ascent that remain to the summit of Les Quatre-Têtes to be tackled with renewed vigour the next day.

From the refuge, continue up the valley, La Combe de Doran, on a well-trodden path, climbing gradually to the Col

The Chaîne des Aravis (north) from Combloux

des Arêtes Noires (Col de Doran). When viewed from the Refuge de Doran, Pointe Percée, totally dominating the vast hollow below, is immensely stirring, a shapely, attractive summit that deservedly carries the appellation 'Cervin des Aravis' – the Matterhorn of Aravis.

The final stages of the boulder and scree slopes leading to the col are a little tedious after the prolonged ascent from Outredière.

The col brings some visual relief at least, and from it continue eastwards (left), climbing a short arête to the summit without further difficulty. The views, not only of the Pointe Percée, but across the Arve valley to the Désert de Platé, and the countless tiny villages that bring life to its slopes, are breathtaking.

Return by the same route to the Refuge de Doran, but, for a speedier descent, take the access road down to Burzier, leaving 1km of road-walking to regain Plan Chevalier.

WALK 72 Col des Annes (1721m: 5646ft), Tête des Annes (1869m: 6132ft) – Unnamed summit (1950m: 6398ft) and Pointe des Delevrets (1966m: 6450ft) – Col de l'Oulettaz (1925m: 6316ft)

Grade:	B/C
Ascent:	918m (3012ft)
Time:	4h 30–5h
Start/Finish:	La Lanche (Le Reposoir)
Map:	IGN 3430 ET: La Clusaz–Grand-Bornand

The Col des Annes boasts a couple of rural chalets/buvettes at which to enjoy a rustic meal in a superb setting, a gîte d'étape, and plenty of parking space for motorised tourists who evidently find the long drive up from Le Grand Bornand to their liking and amusement if the gusto with which they attack their midday meals and the subsequent sprawling about on grassy hillsides is anything to go by.

If, on your visit by the route described here, you decide to have lunch at the Col des Annes, and a pleasant prospect it is, allow me to give you two simple tips, which apply equally to similar situations elsewhere. Firstly, refrain from any form of alcoholic refreshment: in the present instance, what follows needs a steady head and secure footwork. Secondly, always take your meal indoors if there is any suggestion of clouds gathering; the reason is simple: when it starts to rain, everyone rushes indoors balancing plates, half-filled glasses, etc. only to find that, in the main, there were more tables outside than inside. If you are already seated, you will escape the resultant pantomime, and can enjoy it at your leisure!

La Lanche lies at the end of a narrow forest road running south from Le Reposoir, in company with the Petit Foron stream. In Le Reposoir, turn off the main road near the war memorial and follow a metalled road towards Vallon (signposted: 'Carmel'). Ignore the subsequent turning to the Carmelite retreat, a fine and ornate building, and continue, always ahead, to La Lanche, where there is limited roadside parking.

Follow a broad path (signposted: 'Col des Annes') over a nearby bridge and start climbing steadily into forest. Ignore the turning, soon encountered on the left, to Le Vélard (signposted: 'Combe Marto'), and press on to Sommier d'Aval, which you reach just after clearing the forest, and later, to Sommier d'Amont. The ascent through the forest is

En route to the Col des Annes from Le Reposoir

cool and damp, and that, in the heat of July and August, usually means refreshing. Above the forest the pastureland is scrubby, untidy and overgrown, but there is a great variety of wild flowers over which to pass the time.

Shortly after Sommier d'Amont cross a stream, and continue to a junction. Take the signposted route for the Col des Annes, and climb steadily through undergrowth to emerge not far below the col.

From the col, climb south on a steepening pathway to the Tête des Annes, the top of which is also reached by *télésiège* from the Duche valley below, and press on to a slightly higher, but unnamed, top. This proves to be a fine perch from which to inspect the craggy faces of Pointe d'Areu (Walk 76), Pointe Percée (Walk 75), below which it is possible to pick out the Refuge Gramusset, balanced rather precariously, it seems, on a rocky ledge, and Mont Charvet (Walk 82). To the north, the grassy slopes of Pointe d'Almet (Walk 86), stand apart from the limestone massif of the main Chaîne des Aravis, while the distant view takes in the crags of the Pic de Jallouvre (Walk 92), across an intervening ridge.

The direct route onward from the unnamed summit meets a sudden and impassable rock wall overgrown with shrubbery, beyond which you can see the path, a short distance below, passing along the top of a narrow ridge. A short retracing of steps reveals a path around this immediate problem, on the north side, rejoining the ridge at a low col. A fine ridge scamper ensues to the top of Pointe des Delevrets, a narrow summit, with a good view of Pointe d'Areu and its minor relations.

From Pointe des Delevrets, descend with care towards the Col de l'Oulettaz, a short section of the path being along a rickety wooden walkway, and protected by a cable and chains. The col is a tiny gap immediately below Pointe de Rouelletaz, and at this point the walk descends left.

The upper section of the descent from the col is very shaly and slippery. The path is not always evident, and great care is needed, especially after wet weather. Further down the path improves, but there is, in spite of rough Alpine pastures all around, a continuous need for caution until you reach the junction, far below, at which the upward route turned off towards the Col des Annes. From this junction, follow the path back to La Lanche.

WALK 73 Circuit des Annes (Col de l'Oulettaz: 1925m: 6316ft. Pointe de Delevrets: 1966m: 6450ft. Unnamed summit: 1950m: 6398ft. Tête des Annes: 1869m: 6132ft. Col des Annes: 1721m: 5646ft)

Grade:	**B/C**
Ascent:	**780m (2559ft)**
Time:	**4h 30–5h**
Start/Finish:	**Parking area above Les Troncs (Le Grand Bornand)**
Map:	**IGN 3430 ET: La Clusaz–Grand-Bornand**

This fine circular walk around the upper reaches of the Grand Bornand valley is surprisingly popular, and is claimed by some local guidebooks to be 'within the reach of everyone': such generality does not extend to very young children, who might find the stretch between the Col de l'Oulettaz and the Tête des Annes a little intimidating.

From the parking area, take a path heading into forest, and climbing quite strenuously for a while first to reach Plattuy, and, a little more easily, Le Planet. Bilberries grow in profusion around Le Planet, and in August can cause no end of delay.

Leave Le Planet, from where a path ascends brusquely to the Refuge Gramusset, but ignore this, and press on north-eastwards to reach the Col de l'Oulettaz (signposted). At the col, turn left, and follow an ascending path, frail in places, and

At the highest point of the Tête des Annes, facing Pointe d'Areu

protected by cables and chains, to reach the top of the Pointe des Delevrets. A fine ridge, a little shaly in places, runs on from this neat and restricted summit, with the sharp profile of a rocky buttress looming ahead. Just before the buttress, at a shallow col, descend slightly to the right (north) to work a way around the obstruction, doubling back once the ridge is regained to reach its summit, a fine viewpoint.

The ensuing ridge to the Tête des Annes, and the long descent to the Col des Annes, are now straightforward.

From the Col des Annes, take the motorable road downwards for 200m, leaving it then for a rough track which heads for a dip in the woodland that cloaks the western flank of the Tête des Annes. The track continues easily, through the Bois

Aerial view of the Col des Annes

de la Duche, to the Col de Borneronde. Beyond it drops, at first southeastwards, to Plattuy (take care to avoid the turning to Le Planet), from where the final stage of the way down to the parking area will prove far less arduous than it did on the ascent.

WALK 74 Refuge Gramusset (2164m: 7100ft) and Col des Verts (2499m: 8199ft)

Grade:	**B**
Ascent:	**Refuge Gramusset:**
	– from La Lanche: 1073m (3520ft)
	– from Les Troncs: 908m (2979ft)
	– from Col des Annes: 443m (1435ft)
	Col des Verts, from Refuge Gramusset:
	335m (1099ft)
Time:	**Refuge Gramusset:**
	– from La Lanche: 3h–3h 30. Descent: 2h 30
	– from Les Troncs: 3h. Descent: 2h
	– from Col des Annes: 2h 15. Descent: 1h 30
	Col des Verts: 1h 30. Descent: 1h
Start/Finish:	**As indicated above**
Map:	**IGN 3430 ET: La Clusaz–Grand-Bornand**

Although both the Refuge Gramusset and the Col des Verts are worthy excursions in their own right, they are essentially a means to an end; the end is Pointe Percée. The easiest approach is to drive to the Col des Annes and begin the walk from there. The key to approaches from La Lanche and the Col des Annes is the narrow Col de l'Oulettaz, while the ascent from Les Troncs takes a more direct line.

Refuge Gramusset
74a From La Lanche

Follow Walk 72 to the junction at which the route for the Col des Annes goes to the right, and, ignoring this, continue ahead (signposted: 'Refuge Gramusset'), climbing steeply (by the descent given in Walk 72) to the Col de l'Oulettaz. From the col, take a slightly descending path, east of south, to the base of the main limestone massif, and then climb in steep zigzags to the refuge, perched on a broad rocky shelf.

74b From Les Troncs

Follow Walk 73 as far as Le Planet, and from there continue in a steep series of zigzags, roughly eastwards, to meet the path from the Col de l'Oulettaz, finishing in more zigzags to the refuge.

74c From Col des Annes

Use the Col des Annes–Col de l'Oulettaz section of Walk 72, to gain the latter col, and then pursue the description given above.

Col des Verts

Leave the refuge, ascending steeply. The base of Pointe Percée comes down on the left, with a wide, rocky hollow, the Combe des Verts, to the right of it, terminating in rock walls. If the combe is filled with snow, the upper sections can be difficult, and should only be attempted by experienced winter mountaineers. Once the snow has cleared, the way to the col is usually well-trodden, and crosses a massive downspill of scree and boulders, finishing with a steep and airy pull to the col. Some attempt has been made at waymarking, but the route remains less than obvious, and though the terrain is difficult and rocky throughout, the objective is always in sight. This visual reference is important, and the ascent should not be attempted, beyond the refuge, in poor visibility.

Beyond the col, the view opens up across the Arve valley to the Désert de Platé, and the distant Mont Blanc massif.

There is no shortage of clear signposting throughout the lower Alps.

WALK 75 Pointe Percée (2750m: 9022ft)

Not without good cause is Pointe Percée locally described as the 'Matterhorn of Aravis', for, in spite of being more than 1700m (5500ft) less in height than its Swiss counterpart, it has the same distinguished, sharp-edged profile, the same aura of challenge. Unlike the Matterhorn, however, Pointe Percée is less isolated from other mountains, and considerably less demanding. But its ascent ranks among the finest high-mountain excursions away from the Mont Blanc massif, an excursion that will be enhanced by an overnight stay at one of the well-placed refuges, the Doran (Telephone: 50 58 08 00) or the Gramusset (Telephone: 50 02 40 90). The ascent, from either direction, is not for ill-equipped or inexperienced walkers.

Walk 71 describes an ascent to the Refuge de Doran, though a direct approach using the service track from Burzier is quicker, while Walk 74 gives a number of approaches to the Refuge Gramusset. The final route to the summit uses the Crête des Verts, and if the passage on either side of this still retains snow, the ascent should be aborted. Careful attention should also be given to the weather forecast: poor weather, or sudden changes in the wind direction, can make this ascent considerably more difficult.

75a From Refuge de Doran

Grade:	A/B
Ascent:	From Refuge de Doran: 1255m (4117ft)
	From Burzier: 1780m (5840ft)
Time:	Ascent: To the refuge: 1h 30
	Ascent: From the refuge: 4h–4h 30
	Descent: To Burzier: 4h
Map:	IGN 3430 ET: La Clusaz–Grand-Bornand

This approach is without question the most beautiful, and the most dramatic, with the long valley of the Combe de Doran leading the eye to the pyramid of Pointe Percée. Part of the ascent involves advanced scrambling in a quite exposed chimney, followed by a series of rock-strewn ledges, from which there is a constant risk of stonefall. Walkers might benefit from the security of a rope and associated equipment on the chimney section, the summit ridge, and on the descent.

From the Refuge de Doran the ascent begins with a long pull up the Combe de Doran, finishing with tedious boulder and scree slopes to the Col des Arêtes Noires (the Col de Doran). From the col, the route tends towards the right, to begin a rising traverse, quite steep to begin, across mixed slopes of grass and rock (slippery after rain, and to be avoided altogether if covered with snow) beneath the limestone summit. Before the traverse reaches the Crête des Verts, a path doubles back, and leads to the foot of the 'Cheminée de Sallanches', basically a 30m (90–100ft) fissured rock wall, giving access to the arête just south of the summit. The holds, in and either side of the chimney, are comfortingly large, but the sense of exposure is significant, and can prove disconcerting. You may find a rope useful here, where a few fixed pitons and a number of rocky spikes offer security.

On reaching the arête cross to the south flank of the mountain where a series of inclined ledges, laden with loose rocks, lead upwards. If there are parties above this point, take care against stonefall. Higher up, you reach a second arête, and this leads further around, to the west, where you join the ascent from the Refuge Gramusset, and follow it along the final section of the arête, an undulating rocky spine with steep drops on either side, to the summit.

75b From Refuge Gramusset

Grade:	**A/B**
Ascent:	**From the refuge: 617m (2024ft)**
Time:	**Ascent: 2h 30. Descent: 2h**
Map:	**IGN 3430 ET: La Clusaz–Grand-Bornand**

The ascent of Pointe Percée can be comfortably contained within a day if you start from the Col des Annes, reached by a long and serpentine road from the Grand-Bornand valley.

From the refuge a path, worn into the limestone, rises to the base of the first buttresses of Pointe Percée. Here move left, usually towards a bank of névé (ice-axe and crampons essential), and slant across this in a rising traverse to the base of rocks which border it on the right. Great care and judgement is needed here. The snow patches are often hard, and there is a serious risk of stonefall from advance parties.

Climb the rocky ridge ahead, initially climbing left, and later moving right, in the direction of the summit, to reach the base of another buttress. This short passage is also notorious for retaining snow well into summer, and though it seems insignificant, it has a severe reputation. Do not attempt to cross it ill-equipped or without appropriate experience.

Climb the ensuing buttress easily to reach a concave section leading to the summit arête, and meeting the ascent from the Refuge de Doran. Follow the arête left, airy and with a fair degree of exposure, to the summit.

WALK 76 Pointe d'Areu (2462m: 8077ft)

Grade:	A/B
Ascent:	1508m (4947ft)
Time:	Ascent: 5h. Descent: 3h 30
Start/Finish:	Gravin (Magland): road-end above Les Ranziers (Parking, at the start of the forest trail)
Map:	IGN 3430 ET: La Clusaz–Grand Bornand

This summit lies at the end of a formidable line of cliffs running north to south, and overlooking the Arve valley, near Magland. The lower slopes are heavily cloaked in forest, while the upper sections, at this far end of the Chaîne des Aravis, have rather more greenery than the more southerly

Pointe Percée

peaks. On modern maps the nearby summit, Pointe d'Arbennes (2478m), is unnamed, and has long shared the name,
Pointe d'Areu, with its slightly lower, and more easterly
sibling. This ascent, to the lower summit, makes use of an
impressive, and unsuspected, route, the 'Passage du Saix', a
means by which experienced walkers can enjoy steep and
sustained ascent, complex route finding, precarious passages
coupled with significant exposure, and a fine, airy finish. An
ice-axe is essential if any snow remains on the mountain, and a
small length of rope might come in handy in one or two places.

The long and winding road from Gravin eventually terminates at a small parking area, beyond which a forest trail leads
to the Chalets de Mont Ferron, where there is an attractive
oratory. Just after the last chalet, practically on the edge of the
forest, leave the main path, and head right on a narrow GR96
path (waymarked red and white).

After crossing a number of ravines, the path climbs to the
base of broken cliffs, and moves right, on a narrow and tricky
path exposed to stonefall (usually occasioned by chamois or
bouquetins) and cut into the rock. This section, the Passage de
Saix, with steep grassy slopes only a step away, is equipped
with chains provided some years ago by hunters.

Beyond this precarious section the route reaches a rough,
tilted plateau, below the Montagne de Chérente, and from here
the going becomes significantly more difficult and demanding.

Stay on the GR96 for a short while, but when this starts to
ascend towards the ruins of the Chalets de Chérente, leave it,
going left, to reach the Combe Nord d'Areu (shown but not
named on the map). An intervening rocky buttress can be
climbed directly, or passed by, either way leading to a well-
trodden path rising to the foot of a cliff. Continue on this,
below the cliff, in order to reach a grassy slope leading back
above the Passage de Saix. The path continues across a delicate
rocky section before heading for a high rock wall. A steep

lope leads to a narrow gully, unseen from further down, This s the 'Cheminée d'Areu', and it leads to a higher rock platform. Ascent of the chimney is not difficult, and there is an bundance of large holds. At the top of the chimney, it is a good idea to fix its position for the return journey.

Climb the cwm above, at least as far as the start of a boulder nd scree slope, to the right of an almost permanent patch of now. Above, there is a 'gendarme', a fine needle of rock, at an bvious gap, and you can reach it by a grassy ramp. Cross the rèche, and by a little advanced scrambling, reach the final ummit ridge. A short awkward and delicate section follows, efore the final stage, an airy arête, but with no real technical lifficulty.

The summit, not surprisingly, has a fine view across the Arve valley to the towering Aiguilles de Varan, and the Désert le Platé. In spite of the incidence of steep slopes, return by the ame route, avoiding the temptation to descend into the north ombe. This is a far more complex and exposed way down than night seem from the summit, and you should not contemplate t.

WALK 77 Pointe d'Arbennes (2478m: 8130ft)

Grade:	B
Ascent:	1188m (3898ft)
Time:	Ascent: 4h. Descent: 3h
Start/Finish:	Romme-sur-Cluses
Map:	IGN 3430 ET: La Clusaz–Grand-Bornand

Sometimes called, incorrectly, Pointe d'Areu, and unnamed on the IGN map, the Pointe d'Arbennes rises at the north-easterly end of the Chaîne des Aravis. This approach from the pastoral setting of Romme is quite long, but without any sustained ascent in spite of the considerable overall height gain.

The walk begins along the 'dead end' that starts from the southern end of the village, on the left, and about 150m along the road to Le Reposoir. The first objective is the Combe de Vormy, and you can reach either by following the forest trail that winds its way to the Chalets des Vuardes, or by means of a steeper shortcut that sets off beneath the Téléski du Grand Tour. Beyond the chalets, a pleasant path/piste continues to the wide hollow of the Combe de Vormy, hanging high above the Arve valley. There is no particular need to descend to the Chalets de Vormy, since a narrow path sets off along a low ridge on the right (west). This is a little more direct, and avoids losing height unnecessarily, though it does have to drop down a small rock step, and after another slight descent reaches the east side of the Pointe du Château.

Beyond, the path rises to gain a ridge, Le Champ Fleuri, and climbs to the top of a minor summit, the Tête du Château. A broad plateau of Alpine pasture leads to a rocky slope, often covered with snow, which leads, with a final flourish of effort, to the summit of Pointe d'Arbennes.

WALK 78 Tour du massif d'Areu (Tête d'Arbennes: 2478m: 8130ft)

Grade:	**B**
Ascent:	**1524m (5000ft)**
Time:	**8h–9h**
Start/Finish:	**Gravin (Magland): road above Les Ranziers (Parking, at the start of the forest trail)**
Map:	**IGN 3430 ET: La Clusaz–Grand-Bornand**

This is a fine, but neglected, circuit, embracing many different aspects of mountain walking, and having to deal with a varied terrain. Most, but not all, of the route is on prominent paths, nor is all of it waymarked. The walk is essentially a fallback for walkers who want to visit this interesting edge of the Chaîne des Aravis, but without the severe and tiring ascents of Pointe d'Areu (Walk 76). Even so, there are sustained and demanding moments in the first part of the walk, the precarious crossing of the Passage de Saix, and a considerable amount of height gain, putting this outing into the realms of strong and experienced walkers. If snow remains on the higher slopes, an ice-axe will be necessary for the descent of the Couloir de la Forclaz, on which crampons, too, might be found useful early in the season.

You should follow the first part of Walk 76 across the Passage de Saix and, continuing on the GR96 (waymarked red and white), as far as the tilted plateau below the Montagne de Chérente. Here, where Walk 76 sets off southwards to tackle the abruptness of Pointe d'Areu, remain on the GR96, and continue to the ruins of the Chalets de Chérente, now over-grown with wild flowers. Keep heading in the same direction, roughly west of north, until the path climbs to a broad ridge overlooking the vast Combe de Vormy, and here turn left (southwest) on to the ridge. There is no longer much of a footpath, but the line of the ridge is sufficient guide, and leads to a minor top, Le Champ Fleuri, continuing then, as for Walk 77, across the Tête du Château. A platform of easier ground is crossed, and leads to the foot of scree slopes, often covered with snow, ascending ultimately to Pointe d'Arbennes, the highest point of the walk, and a breathtaking viewpoint. Omitting this summit can save up to one and a half hours, and will take 205m (670ft) off the overall ascent.

The next objective is the Col de la Forclaz, between Pointe d'Arbennes and Tête de la Forclaz, and this is most easily reached by retracing your steps down the scree slopes to the easier ground southeast of the Tête du Château, from where the col may be reached.

A long, stony descent ensues, down the Couloir de la Forclaz. Of itself, this is not unduly difficult, though the potential for a slip is considerable. Quite often the couloir is snow-bound, and the upper sections glazed with ice. Half-way down the couloir, a path on the left offers an attractive detour to inspect the Tours d'Areu.

At the foot of the couloir turn left (right for the Refuge de Doran), and begin a long traverse of numerous ravines, with some slight ascent in the first part, to the edge of forest. A good path leads down through the forest to the Chalets de Mont Ferron, where you rejoin the outward route.

WALK 79 Combe des Fours (2128m: 6982ft)

Grade:	**B**
Ascent:	**1128m (3700ft)**
Time:	**5h 30–6h**
Start/Finish:	**Lintre, north side of the Sallanches valley, west of the town**
Map:	**IGN 3430 ET: La Clusaz–Grand Bornand**

A wild, isolated location, populated by chamois, the Combe des Fours offers a long circular walk below the great wall of the Chaîne des Aravis. Backpackers will find the Combe des Fours an ideal camp site, and certain it is that anyone there early in the morning stands the best chance of spotting the chamois that flit across the grassy slopes around the Gouille des Fours, and among the scree and boulders. A smattering of French will translate 'Fours', as 'oven', and with good cause, especially early in the day.

West of Sallanches a minor road climbs into the wooded valley of the Sallanches torrent, and comes effectively to a motorable end near Lintre. Continue on the track to the Pont de la Flée, from where a rough track starts climbing towards the Vallée de Coeur. Follow this as far as La Pierre Fendue (a split boulder), where you encounter the Tour du Pays du Mont Blanc (TPMB). Head northwards on the TPMB for a while, crossing the stream issuing from the Cascade des Fours, and shortly leaving it for a less prominent path (white paint on scattered boulders) heading left towards the base of cliffs. The path then tends to the right to climb through the first barrier at a point of weakness, beyond which there is a steep, grassy slope. Climb this, and begin moving left to pass beneath more cliffs on a slightly exposed path, slippery when wet, to gain the valley above the Cascade des Fours. After a few ascending rocky ledges, cross the stream, and so gain a landscape of Alpine pastures, quite unsuspected after the prolonged rock work below. This is the lower edge of the Combe des Fours, marked by a large boulder, which should be noted by anyone intending to return by the same route.

The lake, the Gouille des Fours, is not visible from this point, but by descending to and crossing the stream, and then following a vague path through the hillocks that surround the lake, its location will eventually be found, though possibly not without frustration and a certain amount of casting about. The nearby minor top, Tête du Gréppon, gives a clue as to its whereabouts, and serves as a fine vantage point over the Sallanches and Arve valleys.

You can return by the same route, but the circular walk given below is much better.

Continue deeper into the combe, tackling a stretch of boggy ground at the southern end, but there finding a waymarked path climbing left, across scree slopes to reach the Col de Portette. Cross the col, and start a long traverse to the base of La Mia, and into the upper section of the Vallée de Cœur, following the ravine of the Torrent de la Miaz. Lower down cross the stream and head for the Chalets de Cœur, having rejoined the TPMB. You now follow this past the Chalets des Frédys to La Lanche du Praz and the Pierre Fendue, when you rejoin the outward route.

WALK 80 Tête Noire (1691m: 5548ft) and Croix du Planet (1838m: 6030ft)

Grade   C+

Ascent:	**628m (2060ft)**
Time:	**4h–5h**
Start/Finish:	**Les Mouilles (Cordon)**
Map:	**IGN 3430 ET: La Clusaz–Grand-Bornand**

Very much a tour of Alpine meadows and forests, this walk makes use of a broad ridge descending northeastwards from the Croise Baulet. This is a popular walk, on good footpaths throughout, though there are a few sustained uphill sections, and the final stage, plagued by ski pistes, can be rather confusing.

The mountain village of Cordon is reached easily from Sallanches, or from Combloux, and by a serpentine road, a parking area near the hamlet of Les Mouilles is ultimately reached.

From the parking area, ignore the track on the left heading for the farm at Le Perret, and take instead another across a meadow, on the right. This leads past a chalet, beyond which it enters forest, and begins a more sustained climb, dealing with the greater part of the ascent early in the walk. You reach a clearing in which repose two chalets, and shortly after these leave the path to climb to the right, to reach the Croix de la Tête Noire, at the northern end of a broad ridge.

From Tête Noire, continue southwest to gain the wide grassy Plateau des Bénés, along which the sound of cow bells will be a constant accompaniment. Press on, past the Chalets des Bénés, climbing gently all the time to reach a small hillock.

Leave the hillock, and begin descending eastwards to reach the Croix du Planet. You can avoid on the left a small rock step just before the summit, before reaching the cross itself.

A steepish descent falls from the Croix du Planet to the upper station of the Téléski de l'Herney. From here a number of onward possibilities, mostly confusing but not unsafe, exist: one heads north, past Les Sions and along the Chemin des Bœufs to the farm at Le Perret; another uses the nearby ski iste to reach a good track leading down to chalets, from where a path (not clearly shown on the map) also ultimately links with the track to Le Perret; yet more penetrate the forests, giving endless permutations. Because of the extensive use of these slopes for skiing, many of the paths become obliterated and/or modified, making clear instructions difficult, since the paths seem to change from year to year. There will be no difficulty in locating Cordon, but take care not to lose too much height if your destination is Les Mouilles.

There is a possibility of extending the walk to reach the Cabane du Petit Pâtre, and descending to Les Seytets (add about one hour), underlining the fact that this is excellent easy-walking country, totally dominated by the towering rocky heights of the Chaîne des Aravis, and with extensive views.

WALK 81 La Miaz (2336m: 7664ft)

Grade	**B +**
Ascent:	**1357m (4452ft)**
Time:	**Ascent: 4h–4h 30. Descent: 3h**
Start/Finish:	**Le Charne (Cordon)**
Map:	**IGN 3430 ET: La Clusaz–Grand Bornand**

Standing slightly apart from the main thrust of the Chaîne des Aravis, La Miaz (sometimes without the 'z'), is a bold and rugged mountain, often neglected in favour of the main ridge. This ascent is not without its difficulties: sustained uphill work, a virtual lack of footpaths in the final stages, and a wild and rough environment, some miles from assistance, in an emergency. From the summit, the scene is one of great contrast: the pastoral Alpine meadows of Cordon on the one hand, and on the other, the harsh severity of the limestone towers of Aravis.

Le Charne lies some way up the slopes that lead ultimately to the Croise Baulet, and is reached by a minor road from Cordon. There is limited parking near by.

The first objective is the Cabane du Petit Pâtre, standing on a col directly north of the Croise Baulet, and reached by a good path that climbs quickly from Le Charne first to the Chalets des Seytets, and then to Les Seytets d'en Haut. The route is uphill all the way, but once at the col some relief is at hand in the form of a slight descent to the Col de Niard.

From the Col de Niard continue roughly in the same direction for a short while, as far as a group of large boulders, one marked with red paint. Pass these, and start climbing left towards the base of La Miaz. The path skirts around a rocky arête and starts to descend into the Vallée de Tré le Crot. At the first grassy terrace abandon the descent (near a large waymarked boulder), and take a moment or two to pinpoint the spot, for the return.

A long grassy ramp now rises towards the summit, running beneath the outcrops of limestone that mark the southern and eastern flanks. There is no significant path here, though one materialises higher up, when the route slants to the right into a small couloir which issues on to a grassy platform directly below the final slopes. Again, take note of the line of ascent just completed, since an error on the return section can lead to a long and circuitous trek.

For the final stages, use a fine arête, a mixture of grass and rock outcrops, on the right, leading to a superb viewpoint from where the Mont Blanc massif for once holds less appeal than the great cliffs and peaks of Aravis.

WALK 82 Mont Charvet (2538m: 8327ft)

Grade:	**B**
Ascent:	**1100m (3609ft)**
Time:	**Ascent: 3h–3h 30. Descent: 2h 30**
Start/Finish:	**Les Confins (La Clusaz) (Parking at road-end)**
Map:	**IGN 3430 ET: La Clusaz–Grand-Bornand**

Very few of the summits of the Chaîne des Aravis are tackled from the east, since from this direction they present a formidable array of cliffs, slippery grass and scree slopes, and rocky buttresses, with few natural weaknesses. Approaches from La Clusaz, however, make life infinitely easier, though, unless you like noisy, bustling towns, La Clusaz itself is not a good base.

Le Mont Charvet lies about 2km (1¼ miles) southwest of Pointe Percée, the highest summit of the range, and is a fine outing, culminating in a shapely peak that dominates the Combe des Fours (Walk 79). Like all the summits of the Aravis range, its ascent is demanding, and involves long stretches of energetic exercise.

From the parking area at Les Confins, take the stony track that leads to the Chalets de la Bottière, then to the Chalet de Paccaly. Continue, in the same direction, into forest, on a more or less horizontal path, and after about 1km (a little over ½ mile) start climbing, to the right, as far as a path junction at which you can go left to gain the base of the Combe de la Forclaz.

A slight descent starts off crossing the Combe de la Forclaz, beyond which a path heads into the Combe du Mont Charvet. Now some real collar-work is needed, climbing into the Combe, and after more than 400m (1310ft) of steady ascent progress is confounded by an enormous cirque of cliffs, below which scree and boulders fan out in endless grey slopes. The possibility of spotting chamois, bouquetin, or marmots enlivens the ascent, but nothing really takes the mind off the unending effort.

More climbing, moving left, takes the route around the great craggy buttresses of La Petite Miaz, a minor peak, towards Mont Charvet and into a high-mountain sanctum from which the only escape is to an obvious brèche (Point 2403) on the main Aravis ridge. Up to this moment, the ascent is relatively straightforward, if strenuous. But the climb to the brèche, and the subsequent rocky ridges leading to a very steep chimney, by means of which you reach the summit, should only be contemplated by walkers experienced in advanced scrambling in exposed situations.

The summit has an extensive view across to the Aiguilles de Varan, the Rochers de Fiz, the Mont Blanc massif and the summits of Beaufortain.

The return is by the same route, and you should exercise great care until you have regained the comparative safety of the Combe du Mont Charvet.

WALK 83 Passage de la Grande Forclaz (2311m: 7582ft)

Grade:	**B**
Ascent:	**870m (2854ft)**
Time:	**Ascent: 3h. Descent: 2h 15**
Start/Finish:	**Les Confins (La Clusaz) (Parking at road-end)**
Map:	**IGN 3430 ET: La Clusaz–Grand Bornand**

The Passage de la Grande Forclaz, a high-mountain pass linking the valleys north of the Chaîne des Aravis with those of the Arve, is a long-established thoroughfare, and at one time frequently used by smugglers. No amount of historical suggestion to the contrary, however, leads anyone struggling up to the pass today to believe this was anything other than a desperate passage even for smugglers used to unconventional routes across the mountains. For modern walkers, rather better equipped, and with maps to guide them, the ascent is not quite so daunting, but no less demanding of effort.

Follow Walk 82 as far as the entrance to the Combe de la Grande Forclaz. Start out into the combe, climbing half right, and after about 300m (1000ft) of ascent, move left towards the centre of this vast rocky hollow. By following the middle ground, not always on a distinct path, you will eventually reach the col. The upper section often retains snow, making an ice-axe essential, but the snow slopes in normal conditions should present no problems to experienced walkers.

WALK 84 Lac de Tardevant (2110m: 6922ft) and L'Ambrevetta (2465m: 8087ft)

Grade:	Lac de Tardevant: B/C
	L'Ambrevetta: B
Ascent:	Lac de Tardevant: 670m (2198ft)
	L'Ambrevetta: 1025m (3363ft)
Time:	Lac de Tardevant: Ascent: 2h. Descent: 1h 45
	L'Ambrevetta: Ascent: 3h–3h 30. Descent:
	2h 15
Start/Finish:	Les Confins (La Clusaz) (Parking at road-end)
Map:	IGN 3430 ET: La Clusaz–Grand-Bornand

The minuscule Lac de Tardevant, snuggled into a hollow carved by an ancient glacier, is a splendid place from which, armed with binoculars, to watch the many chamois and ptarmigan that frequent this high corrie valley. It makes a worthy objective for a walk in itself.

The first stage of this walk, perhaps as far as the lake, is not unduly difficult, and, being nearer to the road-end at Les Confins, tends to receive more attention. Beyond the lake, the route enters the preserve of experienced mountaineers, becoming considerably steeper, prone to stonefall, and, if snow is present, demands the use of an ice-axe.

From the parking area at Les Confins take the stony track leading to the Chalet de la Lanchette, the Chalets de la Bottière and Paccaly. From Paccaly take a path on the right which soon swings round to cross the base of the Combe de Paccaly.

Continue past the Chalet Paccaly d'en Haut to reach the Combe de Tardevant and its chalets, taking care not to go too far along the traversing path, which hastens on to combes further up the main valley. Now ascend the combe, more or less in its centre, on a distinct path that finally zigzags up to the lake.

Beyond the lake, the slopes steepen considerably, climbing to a headwall of cliffs. By moving to the left as it approaches the headwall, the route, which becomes less obvious with height, passes between two large boulders, among many, and reaches the main ridge by a steep final flourish. Note the point at which you reach the ridge. A fairly straightforward, but airy and scrambly arête then leads to the summit of L'Ambrevetta.

Walkers with energy to spare might consider following the ascending ridge to the northwest to include the Pointe de Tardevant, which is slightly higher than L'Ambrevetta. Neither the distance nor the ascent is much of an imposition, but the terrain is very rugged, the route not always evident, and progress demands concentration at all times.

You will need to take great care descending from the ridge back into the Combe de Tardevant.

WALK 85 Trou de la Mouche (2453m: 8048ft)

Grade:	**B**
Ascent:	**1013m (3323ft)**
Time:	**Ascent: 3h. Descent: 2h 30**
Start/Finish:	**Les Confins (La Clusaz) (Parking at the road-end)**
Map:	**IGN 3430 ET: La Clusaz–Grand-Bornand**

An unexpected linking between the Combe du Grand Crêt and the Combe de Paccaly, the Trou de la Mouche is a natural tunnel, high on the main ridge of the Chaîne des Aravis. The complete passage, from one combe to the other, is accessible only to experienced walkers, equipped at least with an ice-axe if snow remains on the high slopes, though less experienced walkers can access either combe without too much difficulty.

The scenery, as in all these Aravis combes, is magnificent: grey–green and brown slopes from which lofty limestone peaks reach skywards, the occasional pine tree, isolated from the many that otherwise afforest the lower slopes, and the ever present panorama of snow-capped peaks and distant green hills. Independent chalets, many occupied during the summer months by shepherds on their lonely vigil, dot the landscape, and provide the opportunity to engage in dialect conversation and buy home-made cheeses.

From the parking area at Les Confins, take the stony track leading to the Chalet de la Lanchette, and, in due course, that at Paccaly. There, a narrow path on the right sets off to traverse the lower slopes of the combe, until it reaches the chalet at Paccaly d'en Haut. From here, another path now climbs into the Combe de Paccaly (waymarked), and, though not always immediately obvious it slowly works a way through and around numerous small hillocks, each one raising hopes that it will be the last. Eventually, the ascent, which is sustained throughout, reaches a short-lived easing of the gradient beneath a great spill of scree. From here the route heads towards the conspicuous Tête de Paccaly in order to turn a high rock barrier, known as the Passage du Père. The going is particularly arduous for a while, battling with scree and boulders, but the recompense, on reaching the main ridge is great. Now awaits one of the finest views in the Alps, extending from the Aiguille Verte, across the countless Chamonix aiguilles, to Mont Maudit and the Dômes de Miage. The immediate comparison, too, between the two sides of the Chaîne des Aravis is most dramatic.

Now, by an airy and exposed traverse, a final 'walk' leads to the Trou de la Mouche, which penetrates the Roche Perfia: it is a quite spectacular and unique situation.

Once through the 'hole', the first few steps of the descent into the Combe du Grand Crêt require considerable care, but then all that remains is a straightforward serpentine descent of the combe, before long reaching grassy slopes which rejoin the outward route not far from La Lanchette.

WALK 86 Pointe de Grande Combe (2210m: 7251ft and 2223m: 7510ft) and Pointe d'Almet (2232m: 7323ft)

Grade:	**B –**
Ascent:	**570m (1870ft)**
Time:	**Ascent: 2h. Descent: 1h 30**
Start/Finish:	**Col des Annes**
Map:	**IGN 3430 ET: La Clusaz–Grand-Bornand**

Although approachable by a long and artificial route from the Col de la Colombière, Pointe d'Almet and its near neighbour are most easily ascended from the Col des Annes. This approach does involve some very strenuous uphill work, but throughout the ascent there is a compensating view of the Chaîne des Aravis, and the knowledge that a steady uphill plod technique will succeed in reaching what proves to be a fine summit ridge.

You can drive to the Col des Annes by a long and serpentine road originating in Le Grand-Bornand, and this is by far the easiest way. An alternative, well worthy of consideration by walkers who can afford (time, not expense) to stay overnight at one of the chalets at the Col des Annes, is to use the ascent described in Walk 72. On a fine evening, the setting sun turns the limestone-grey cliffs of the Pointe Percée every conceivable shade of red; to sit and watch it happen from the col, perhaps further coloured by a bottle of local wine, is a truly memorable experience. True, you could motor up and watch the sun set, but when it has, the subsequent drive down in gathering darkness is hairy . . . believe me!

From the Col des Annes a broad track heads for the hollow below the two summits. Quite early on, a path goes left to reach the south ridge of Pointe de Grande Combe, and you can

Pointe d'Almet rises steeply above the Col des Annes

use this. Alternatively, continue up towards the combe for a while longer, aiming to the left of a small gully, and reach the grassy bar that forms the combe. Go left along this minor ridge to join the south ridge as before. Now climb steeply upwards, always on grass, to reach the summit, where a little rock pokes from the otherwise green landscape.

Press on a short distance northwards to the slightly higher, but unnamed point (2223m), and there follow the main ridge east in splendid fashion to Pointe d'Almet.

The view northwards, of the Chaîne de Bargy, is almost as fine a prospect – some would say considerably better – as that to the south. Either way, Pointe d'Almet is a worthy summit from which to make your mind up. Return by the same route.

WALK 87 Sentier du Pas du Roc (1395m: 4577ft)

Grade:	**C+**
Ascent:	**475m (1558ft)**
Time:	**4h**
Start/Finish:	**Stèle (Thorens-Glières)**
Map:	**IGN 3430 ET: La Clusaz–Grand-Bornand**

The great massif of Bornes is a collection of high limestone plateaux and peaks, delineated to the north and the east by the Arve, to the southeast by the Arly, and to the south by the valley of La Chaise. To the west, its boundaries flow down to the lake at Annecy. It is a place where soft pastoral loveliness meets penetrating limestone peaks, bound together by the ever present flow of countless streams and cascades.

The Sentier du Pas du Roc is a means of reaching a hidden pastoral retreat, where, so the local farmers claim, the grass is rich in milk, and a pair of binoculars is an indispensable item of walking equipment. This vast green arena, where silence is unknown and the hillsides are invested with the ringing tonality of cowbells, lies south of another famed region, the Montagne de Sous-Dine (Walk 88).

Finding the start of the walk is a little confusing, and requires a motoring atlas, since the IGN map for the area, although showing the complete route, does not reveal the approach roads. From Thorens-Glières take the road to Usillon. After Nant-Sec, take the road on the left to the Plateau des Glières, and about 2km (just over a mile) later, just after crossing the torrent that flows and prominently cascades from the north side of Sous-Dine, locate a parking area built a little further, on both sides of the road.

Return along the road until about 100m before the bridge, to the signposted start of the Sentier du Pas du Roc. The route throughout is clear, with little prospect of going wrong, and the nearby cascade is a splendid sight. To the left of the stream a path sets off into spruce woodland and climbs in wide zigzags to reach the cliff over which the cascade falls.

The path is far from a natural line, tackling the cliff wall by a man-made ledge carved across its face, but it is one of the most delightful paths in the Bornes massif. Completely open on one side, the path is protected on the other by a chain, though none is really needed, and leads to a tunnel constructed around 1830 to meet the needs of a glass manufacturing industry once thriving in the valley below. Ironically, given the effort that went into constructing the tunnel and its pathways, the glass industry lasted a mere 30 years. The tunnel, however, remained a popular thoroughfare, and subsequently served the needs of smugglers, shepherds, and even members of the French Resistance during the Second World War. The floor of the tunnel is 'paved' with logs, and only a short walk remains beyond it to reach the edge of the Champ Laitier. A path, and a bridge across the top of the cascade, lead through a wooded valley to the Alpine meadows beyond.

How far you progress up the Champ Laitier is a matter of choice; but the area abounds in wildlife, notably chamois (more than 600 have been counted in and around the plateau), black grouse, golden eagle, and lynx . . . and Alpine chalets, almost forty of them, all occupied during the summer months. If you can cope with the constant clatter of cowbells, the Champ Laitier is a splendid place to explore, and ideal for a picnic.

WALK 88 Montagne de Sous-Dine (2004m: 6575ft)

Grade:	C + +
Ascent:	1057m (3468ft)
Time:	5h 30–6h
Start/Finish:	Stèle (Thorens-Glières)
Map:	IGN 3430 ET: La Clusaz–Grand-Bornand

The Montagne de Sous-Dine is an immense limestone plateau superbly designed, it would seem, for losing one's way on. It lies within the vast regional forest of Haute Fillière, though the mountain itself is virtually devoid of trees.

Walk 87 (the Sentier du Pas du Roc) should be used to gain the Champ Laitier, heading up the valley on a path that ultimately leads to the Col de l'Ébat. Long before this, as the first cliffs of Sous-Dine appear ahead on the left, take a path going left to the Chalet de Landron.

Pass behind the chalet, and start to climb the slope beyond at an oblique angle, gradually working a way around the steeper slopes to gain a path returning in an easterly direction into a very broad gully. The onward route (this is but one of numerous possibilities) eventually starts changing direction, now going northeast to cross the centre of the plateau, and continuing steadfastly towards its northern extremity. There are paths covering most of the route, though they become difficult to follow at times, until they re-appear in the centre of the plateau: it is often a case of either too much choice, or none at all. A vast assortment of bumps and hollows lowers the art of navigation to the status of guesswork, known in nautical circles as dead-reckoning, but, since the perimeter of the plateau is ringed by sizeable cliffs, any significant deviation from the general north-easterly direction will be noticed, sooner or later.

Whether you find the highest point or not, come back by the same route.

WALK 89 Pointe d'Andey (1877m: 6158ft)

Grade	C/D
Ascent:	375m (1230ft)
Time:	Ascent: 1h–1h 30. Descent: 0h 45–1h
Start/Finish:	Solaison (Mont-Saxonnex)
Map:	IGN 3430 ET: La Clusaz–Grand-Bornand

Here is a walk for all the family, from the youngest to the oldest; a simple, straightforward ascent, and not much of that, to a summit with a fine view of the group of mountains north of Taninges, notably the Roc d'Enfer (Walk 13) and the Pointe du Marcelly (Walks 26 and 27), of Le Môle (Walk 29), and to the southwest, the great cliffs of Sur-Cou and the Montagne de Sous-Dine (Walk 88).

Solaison is a remote mountain village, reached either from Thuet or Mont-Saxonnex, through the village of Brizon. From the village the summit lies northwest, and is reached by a simple and very direct path, well trodden, across grassy slopes. This is all the direction you will need.

When the summit, surmounted by an iron cross and a statue, is reached the vertical cliffs of the north face become suddenly evident, and a little caution is needed. Although the map appears to indicate a firing range I myself have never seen any signs of military activity. Return by the same route.

WALK 90 Tour des Rochers de Leschaux (Col de Cenise: 1724m: 5656ft)

Grade	C/D
Ascent:	222m (728ft)
Time:	3h–3h 30
Start/Finish:	Solaison (Mont-Saxonnex)
Map:	IGN 3430 ET: La Clusaz–Grand-Bornand

Not unlike the Montagne de Sous-Dine in structure, the Rochers de Leschaux, in themselves of little interest, being rather fragmented and confusing, nevertheless provide the excuse to effect a circular walk in a very relaxed setting where all that is needed is a warm, sunny day and a quiet, reflective outlook on life.

From Solaison take the wide track that sets off southeast and heads for a nearby forest. The path leads to a passage between the Rochers de Leschaux and Les Combes, and continues to the flat Alpine meadows of the Plateau de Cenise. This is a spot much favoured by campers, and is a very agreeable setting, from which to gaze across to the craggy, and far more demanding, summits of the two Bargys and the Pic de Jallouvre.

Cross a wide meadow to reach a broad track, at the Col de Cenise (though the description 'Col', for what is a broad pastural expanse, is heavy with linguistic licence). The track is motorable by off-the-road vehicles and links Morsulaz and Le Petit-Bornand–Les Glières.

Continue southwest, down the track to a chalet/buvette (Point 1617), and from there take a contouring path to Les Gérats. The crags of Leschaux are now directly above, and by traversing the grassy slopes beneath them, heading north, the path eventually reaches the foot of the crags, here popular with novice rock climbers.

Press on across a sloping balcony between the main Rochers de Leschaux, and those of Leschaux inférieurs. Ahead the view opens up of the vallée du Petit-Bornand and the distant flatlands of St Pierre-en-Faucigny.

Soon, the path turns to the right, bringing Solaison back into view beyond a plateau of rock outcrops and grassy islands. Only a simple descending stroll remains to reach the village.

WALK 91 Lac de Lessy (1730m: 5676ft. Col de Sosay: 2052m: 6732ft)

Grade:	**B**
Ascent:	**Outward: 572m (1876ft): Return: 322m (1056ft)**
Time:	**5h–6h**
Start/Finish:	**Solaison (Mont-Saxonnex)**
Map:	**IGN 3430 ET: La Clusaz–Grand-Bornand**

The advantage of starting this walk at Solaison is that you can make a variant on the return journey to pass around the Rochers de Leschaux from the Col de Cenise (see Walk 90).

An alternative starting-point is at Les Frachets, at the end of the road Mont-Saxonnex–Morsulaz–Les Frachets, from where a broad track climbs easily to the Col de Cenise. This variant start would reduce the overall ascent by 130m (425ft), and save a little on time.

Follow Walk 90 from Solaison as far as the Col de Cenise from where a path leaves the broad track and heads directly south, aiming for the conspicuous summit of the Pic de Jallouvre. This shortly climbs a little and curves round, in line with the Arête de Chevry, to reach the foot of a rock wall. Continue below the wall until it becomes possible to climb above it by a short passage equipped with cables, but not unduly awkward.

Above the rock wall, the route ascends into an attractive combe dominated by the Pic de Jallouvre and its near neighbour, Pointe Blanche. Across the combe a rocky path traversing boulder slopes reaches the Col de Sosay, a gap in the northwest ridge of the Pic de Jallouvre. The final few strides to the col are exposed, and rather more intimidating than might be expected. Take care here.

From the col, the Lac de Lessy is in view directly below, to which the route now descends, at first by steep slopes, and then by easier ground. Nearby chalets provide welcome refreshments, and accommodation.

Return by the same route, taking care in the vicinity of the Col de Sosay and on leaving the subsequent combe for the Plateau de Cenise. If returning to Solaison, consider the merit of varying the finish by touring the Rochers de Leschaux. This will add about an hour to the journey.

WALK 92 Pic de Jallouvre (2408m: 7900ft) and Pointe Blanche (2438m: 7998ft)

Grade:	A/B
Ascent:	1026m (3366ft)

Time:	Ascent: Pic de Jallouvre: 3h. Pointe Blanche: + 1h Descent: 2h–2h 30
Start/Finish:	Les Frachets (Morsulaz: Mont-Saxonnex)
Map:	IGN 3430 ET: La Clusaz–Grand-Bornand

Given that the ascent to Pic de Jallouvre uses a high-mountain pass, the Col du Rasoir, between the summit and Pointe Blanche, it seems sensible to combine the two peaks in one outing. To do so, however, demands considerable fitness. Even without this combination, the ascent of either summit is only within reach of experienced walkers with the ability to scramble confidently in exposed situations. You might find it useful to have a short length of rope, and associated equipment, at a few points on Pointe Blanche.

Pic de Jallouvre and Pointe Blanche from Col de Cenise

By following the road from Mont-Saxonnex to Morsulaz, by-passing the tempting restaurant there serving regional specialities, you eventually arrive at the lower edge of the Plateau de Cenise, at Les Frachets. A simple and broad track, motorable by off-the-road vehicles, leads easily from Les Frachets to the Col de Cenise.

At the col leave the broad trail and head due south, curving round with the Arête de Chevry, and later approaching a rock wall at the lower limit of the Combe-Nord du Jallouvre. Towards the middle of the wall, a weakness, equipped with cables, enables passage into the combe above. Press on, climbing into the combe to a path junction. To the right lies the route to the Col de Sosay and Lac de Lessy (Walk 91), but leave this, and continue climbing steeply – even more so as you pass around a grassy moraine to gain the boulder and scree slopes above. By ascending these the route finally reaches the Col du Rasoir, with a fine view south to the Chaîne des Aravis.

At the col turn right (southwest), and follow a narrow arête, not as razor-edged as the name of its col might lead one to believe, but still demanding the utmost care and attention. The Pic de Jallouvre looms ahead, rising above the ridge in a daunting challenge. If snow is visible on the final slopes of Jallouvre, the only sensible option is to retreat, since in such conditions the summital cone has a serious reputation.

From the end of the ridge a long traverse ensues, staying beneath the summit, and moving round the peak to gain the west ridge. It is this section which is notoriously dangerous if snow or ice is present. Moreover, on this long traverse, there is also the risk of stonefall, not so much from walkers above, but from bouquetin. Once you reach the west ridge, a good path, airy and exposed but easy, leads finally to the summit.

To descend, or to continue to Pointe Blanche, retreat, with great care, to the Col du Rasoir.

For Pointe Blanche, the ascent of which will have stared you

Lac Bénit

---

in the face for some time, though you may not have had much opportunity to study it, follow a waymarked route from the Col du Rasoir, which starts off traversing horizontally for a short distance. Soon, the path surmounts a rock step on the left, and then crosses a ravine at the top of an ascent from the Col de la Colombière. Take especial care here not to dislodge stones.

Continue traversing and ascending slightly to the foot of a rock wall situated directly beneath the summit. There continue climbing, scrambling over rocky slabs, to reach a sloping terrace giving access to a slight dip in this final summit ridge. The remainder of the ridge leads without difficulty to the small cross on the summit.

You need to take considerable care on the descent, particularly of the rock slabs. Again, if snow is present, do not contemplate completing the ascent.

WALK 93 Lac Bénit (1450m: 4757ft. Col de l'Anténiou: 1570: 5150ft)

Grade:	**C**
Ascent:	**350m (1148ft)**
Time:	**Ascent: 1h–1h 30. Descent: 1h**
Start/Finish:	**Morsulaz (Mont-Saxonnex)**
Map:	**IGN 3430 ET: La Clusaz–Grand-Bornand**

Pressed tightly against the vertical cliffs of Le Petit Bargy, Lac Bénit proves, especially at weekends, to be a popular place from which to enjoy the antics of rock climbers. It is a sombre place early in the day, but when the sun finally rises above the limestone walls that shade it, the lake takes on a magical sparkle, and comes very much alive, its iridescent green hues contrasting markedly with the dark-shaded conifers and the pale grey limestone all around. A chalet/buvette on its shores, and an apparent abundance of fish, simply add to the appeal.

Begin from near the lower station of the Télésiège de Morsulaz, where there is ample room to park. Follow a path (waymarked) around a field boundary to a nearby building, and there pursue a sheltered path through undergrowth. Soon this breaks out to ascend open ground, and moves generally left, below the lower cliffs of Le Grand Bargy. A short steep section, a little eroded in places, climbs to a small platform near the top of the *télésiège*, and here the lake springs into view 120m (390ft) below. The great cliffs of Le Petit Bargy are also impressive, and on the cliff face it is possible to make out two large 'holes' separated by a rock pillar: these, imaginatively, are the 'Eyes' and the 'Nose' of Petit Bargy.

From the platform, a path zigzags down to the western end of the lake, allowing walkers heading for Le Petit and Le

*The route to the Petit and Grand Bargy tackles the scree slope at the
far end (left) of the lake*

Grand Bargy to gain a foothold on the scree slopes leading to the Col d'Encrenaz. An easier option, left, keeps to the high ground above the lake, and fashions a pleasant descent through sparse woodland that hosts, among other birds, nutcrackers and green woodpeckers. As a track appears on the right, take it, and from a bend, descend directly to the lake on a narrow path.

A path works a way around the lake, and you can return by the ascending zigzag path at the western end.

An alternative descent is to return to the broad track above the lake and follow this northwards, and later head northwest to descend through woodland to Le Bété. This leaves a stroll of about 1km (½ mile) back to Morsulaz. This will add about half an hour to the overall time. It follows, of course, that this resultant circuit can be reversed. There is a car park at Le Bété.

WALK 94 Le Petit Bargy (2098m: 6883ft)

Grade:	B
Ascent:	938m (3077ft)
Time:	Ascent: 3h–3h 30. Descent: 2h 30
Start/Finish:	Le Bété (Mont-Saxonnex)
Map:	IGN 3430 ET: La Clusaz–Grand-Bornand

Although you may start this ascent just as easily from Morsulaz (see Walk 93), you lose a good slice of the ascent from that direction in the descent to Lac Bénit, only to regain it later. The longer ascent from Le Bété is more gradual, and loses only a little height in the process as it, too, descends to the lake.

From the direction of Mont-Saxonnex, you reach the car park at Le Bété by a sharp left turn just as you arrive at the first buildings, and it is not immediately obvious. From it, a path winds upwards through woodland to reach open meadows at Malacquis, and continues gently to arrive at a bend overlooking Lac Bénit, with the great walls of Le Petit Bargy in view directly ahead for most of the way.

Descend from the bend to the lake, and follow a path on the right around the northern shore to reach the foot of the conspicuous broad scree-filled couloir separating the two Bargys. A zigzagging path works a steep way up the scree to a rock wall; this path is notoriously loose and can be dangerous in wet conditions. It is used as a descent each August by competitors in a gruelling trans-Aravis-Borne mountain guides race that is tremendously satisfying . . . to watch!

The rock wall is dealt with by a steep and airy path leading to a slanting and rocky pull to the Col d'Encrenaz. From the col ascend left (east) on comparatively easy rock to the plateau-like summit.

WALK 95 Le Grand Bargy (2301m: 7549ft)

Grade:	**B+**
Ascent:	**1140m (3740ft)**
Time:	**Ascent: 3h 30–4h. Descent: 2h 30–3h**
Start/Finish	**Le Bété (Mont-Saxonnex)**
Map:	**IGN 3430 ET: La Clusaz–Grand-Bornand**

A rather different proposition than the ascent of Le Petit Bargy, though both summits share the same ascent as far as the Col d'Encrenaz. Le Grand Bargy, from the col, concludes with a superb, undulating rocky ridge that is as entertaining as any in the Aravis-Borne-Bargy region.

Follow Walk 94 to the Col d'Encrenaz, and there turn right (southwest) to begin a long traverse across a limestone crest, dealing en route with many small summits around which the safest way is usually waymarked with paint. The traverse is fairly straightforward, but demands the aptitude of experienced walkers with scrambling ability.

Le Grand Bargy

WALK 96 Les Trois Aiguilles (Pointe de Mandallaz: 2277m: 7470ft)

Grade:	**B**
Ascent:	**1107m (3631ft)**
Time:	**Ascent: 3h 30. Descent: 2h 30**
Start/Finish:	**Sous l'Aiguille (Manigod: Tournance)**
Map:	**IGN 3531 OT: Megève–Col des Aravis**

Viewed from the touristy Col des Aravis, the rocky tower of L'Étale is enough to deter anyone, but behind it, out of sight, a fine ridge, a natural extension of the Chaîne des Aravis, flows on. Presenting, as it does, a steep rocky profile to the south and east, most ascents along this ridge are made via the easier western flanks, reached from the popular resorts of La Clusaz and Thônes.

The ascent of Les Trois Aiguilles, also known as Pointe de Mandallaz, makes use of a narrow, wooded valley south and east of Thônes, passing first through the mountain villages of Manigod, Tournance and La Gutary. Culminating in a fine view of the massifs of Mont Blanc and Beaufortain, the ascent, a beautiful excursion, is generally without difficulty, but involves some strenuous exercise.

From Sous l'Aiguille take the forest trail that runs on beyond the road-end, and cross the stream, the Fier, which here in all modesty cascades pleasantly from the summital slopes of Mont Charvin, later to join forces with the mighty Rhône.

Continue to the forest's upper limit, and follow the path across Alpine meadows, much ravined and dotted with large boulders, as it swings round beneath La Tulle to a junction of pathways. This whole region is renowned for its variety of wild flowers, which not even those destined earnestly for the tops can ignore: martagon lilies, gentian and anemones flourish here in great profusion, benefiting from the warmth and shelter given by the circle of mountains above.

Shortly, the path descends to recross the Fier, and continues, generally in a north easterly direction towards the Chalet de l'Aulp de Fier d'en Bas, visible in the distance. From the chalet a horizontal path leads on for a while before climbing once more as it ascends the combe north of Tête de l'Aulp, the Champ Tardif. Grassy, bouldered slopes lead to a small lake, the Lac du Champ Tardif, and on to reach the main ridge, along which, travelling northeast, you reach the summit of Les Trois Aiguilles without difficulty.

To the north of the summit, the long ridge continues, but narrows dramatically and is impractical for all but the most experienced mountaineers. The safest return is by the outward

The prospect west from the Col des Aravis

route, but, shortly after the Lac du Champ Tardif, a path slips off, left, to reach l'Aulp de Fier d'en Haut, from where there is a fine view of the pyramid of Mont Charvin (Walk 98), and you can use this minor variant to add a little more interest to an already delightful walk. From l'Aulp de Fier d'en Haut a good path leads down to the path junction encountered on the ascent, and so back to Sous l'Aiguille.

WALK 97 Lac du Mont Charvin (2011m: 6598ft. Intervening ridge: 2070m: 6791ft)

Grade:	C+
Ascent:	900m (2953ft)
Time:	Ascent: 3h. Descent: 2h 30

Start/Finish: Sous l'Aiguille (Manigod: Tournance)
Map: IGN 3531 OT: Megève–Col des Aravis

One of by far the most beautiful walks in the region, the ascent to Lac du Mont Charvin, high in a mountain corrie, benefits from an early start. The corrie is very much a heat trap, to which the wealth and variety of wild flowers found carpeting the meadows will testify. An early start might also bring an encounter with chamois, which later in the day prefer the shelter of the forest.

Follow Walk 96 as far as the junction of pathways, near the Fier stream. From this point, do not cross the stream but continue by the variant descent given in that walk, on a good path ascending across meadows liberally dotted with boulders, to the Chalet de l'Aulp de Fier d'en Haut. Continue past the chalet, shortly turning southwards to tackle a brief steep section, crossing a rocky barrier plunging from the minor summit, La Goenne.

The path now runs horizontal for a while, rising steadily directly beneath the northern slopes of Mont Charvin, and crossing mixed ground of rich green meadow and rock barriers, all easy to climb, before reaching the lip of a crater in which the lake rests.

The lake is dominated by the towering 400m (1300ft) walls of Mont Charvin, and is a most exquisite setting, reflecting the surrounding peaks.

A little more effort will bring within reach the main ridge, a short distance beyond the lake. This optional extension leads to arguably one of the finest viewpoints in the French Alps; it will add about 1h–1h 30 in total to the walk.

WALK 98 Mont Charvin (2409m: 7903ft)

Grade: B +
Ascent: 924m (3031ft)
Time: Ascent: 3h. Descent: 2h

Start/Finish: Les Fontanettes (La Savatte: Le Bouchet)
Map: IGN 3531 OT: Megève–Col des Aravis

Capable of ascent from Sous l'Aiguille, but only by experienced mountaineers with considerable scrambling skills, bordering on rock climbing, Le Mont Charvin offers a less demanding alternative from the Chaise valley.

Skilled walkers preferring the northern approach should follow Walks 96 and 97 as far as Lac du Mont Charvin, then continuing, as described in Walk 97, to the main ridge. What follows, first south and then west, to reach the summit is a narrow arête, very exposed, with steep drops on both sides, not a place for the faint-hearted.

Lesser mortals, or those for whom discretion is the keystone of survival, should thread their way from Thônes, south on the D12 to Serraval, and then on to the village of Le Bouchet. From Le Bouchet take the road for the Col de l'Épine for a short distance, then leave it before crossing the river, near a sawmill, there turning left for La Savatte. Continue to Les Fontanettes, where you may park the car.

Much of this ascent is across open mountainside, and is a far cry from the pastoral beauty to the north of the mountain. But it is enlivened by the presence of numerous grouse and, flitting along the cliff faces, wallcreepers, the latter, rarely found in Britain, a most beautiful grey bird with red and black wings.

From Les Fontanettes a rough track runs east and climbs to the Chalet/buvette du Haut de Marlens. Already Mont Charvin seems close at hand, but this illusion will take a few hours of walking to dispel. Beyond the chalet a path continues in an easterly direction, shortly descending into a broad valley populated with marmots. Descend into the valley, at its lowest point meeting a path from the Col des Porthets, and then continue beneath some rock outcrops to reach the foot of a very steep slope soaring up to the summit.

The terrain is a mixture of grassy slopes and stony/rocky sections, and prone to stonefall from inconsiderate walkers above. A seemingly unending series of zigzags ploughs up the mountainside, finally reaching the northwest ridge of Mont Charvin, with yet more ascent in store. Thankfully, all that remains is a straightforward, if energetic, pull to a summit marked by a triangulation point.

The view is breathtaking, and a splendid reward for sustained effort and determination.

WALK 99 Tour de la Tulle (Le Freu: 1683m: 5522ft – Col des Porthets: 2072m: 6798ft)

Grade:	**B**
Ascent:	**928m (3045ft)**
Time:	**5h–6h**
Start/Finish:	**Sous l'Aiguille (Manigod: Tournance)**
Map:	**IGN 3531 OT: Megève–Col des Aravis**

This circuit of a mountain dominated by a much superior neighbour is rather more demanding (and commensurately rewarding) than might be supposed, taking walkers through a range of interesting features embracing geology, flora and fauna, and the strictures of an Alpine economy. The opportunity to study, albeit cursorily, these fascinating aspects of the French Alps should not be ignored.

Sections of the walk, notably near the Col des Porthets, are notoriously slippery and dangerous, and should not be contemplated by inexperienced walkers. The whole route travels much of the ground covered in the three preceding walks, but does so in one outing.

From Sous l'Aiguille continue southwards into the forest, ascending on a prominent path to a junction, just above the Fier stream. Here, a path doubles back and ascends grassy slopes towards a couple of stands of spruce, crossing a number of minor rock steps in the process, and finally using the bed of a stream to reach the ridge north of La Tulle, at Le Freu. This first section of the walk is not in good condition underfoot, and you need great care to avoid a slip.

From the pasture at Le Freu, descend westwards for a short distance to reach the GR de Pays Tournette-Aravis, heading southwest, which you leave left after about 500m. Continue now on a gently rising path which turns the west ridge of La Tulle, and eventually swings round to head for the Chalet/ buvette du Haut de Marlens.

Ascend eastwards from the chalet and then drop into a broad valley, at its lowest point branching left to climb steeply in zigzags to the Col des Porthets. Beyond the col, where care is needed, descend to cross the upper reaches of the Fier stream, and then, rising slightly, press on to meet the path that descends from Lac du Mont Charvin (Walk 97). The subsequent descent is fairly straightforward, calling first at the Chalet de l'Aulp de Fier d'en Haut before rejoining the outward route at the path junction.

Early in the morning, and in the evening, many of the slopes are frequented by chamois, while the slopes to the south of the Col des Porthets are populated by marmots.

WALK 100 Pointe d'Orsière (1750m: 5741ft)

Grade:	C
Ascent:	**790m (2592ft)**
Time:	**Ascent: 2h 30. Descent: 2h**
Start/Finish:	**La Gutary (Manigod: Tournance)**
Map:	**IGN 3531 OT: Megève–Col des Aravis**

With numerous variant possibilities making use of forest trails, the ascent of Pointe d'Orsière is a pleasant walk, culminating in a neat summit overlooking the Fier valley, from which it begins.

In La Gutary, take the path crossing the Fier stream, and head immediately into forest, climbing steeply in zigzags to a clearing containing the Chalet de la Balme. From the chalet, continue in a southerly direction, re-entering forest and climbing, without the aid of zigzags, to another clearing, at Le Crozet. Another short stretch of forest leads to its upper limit, beyond which easy grassy slopes lead first to Le Macheux, and then on to the summit of Pointe d'Orsière.

The forest below shelters not only the chamois that frequent the open slopes in the early morning and late in the evening, but wild boar, too, though they are extremely difficult to find.

USEFUL ADDRESSES AND ORGANISATIONS

CIMES (Centre Information Massifs et Sentiers), 7, rue Voltaire, 38000 GRENOBLE (Tel: 76 51 76 00)

Information about walking in the Alps (including accommodation, routes, general advice, programme of walks, etc.)

Club Alpin Français, 24, avenue de Laumière, 75019 PARIS (Tel: 42 02 75 94)

Club Alpin Français, Chalet d'Accueil, Avenue Michel-Croz, 74400 CHAMONIX-MONT-BLANC (Tel: 50 53 16 03)

Fédération Française de la Randonnée Pédestre, 9, avenue George V, 75008 PARIS (Tel: 47 23 62 32)

Produces magazine: *Randonnée*, Catalogues of GRs (Long Distance Footpaths), and IGN maps, plus a mass of information on walking in France

French Government Tourist Office, 178 Piccadilly, LONDON, W1V 0AL (Tel: 071 491 7622)

Holds an enormous amount of information about every aspect of travel in France. Useful publications include *The Traveller in France: Reference Guide* and the *Touring Traveller in France*, plus an annual guide to the Logis de France.